So You Have This
Opportunity

Get Going Again When You Lose Your Job

Dr. Bob Robison

ARCHWAY
PUBLISHING

This book is a work of non-fiction. Unless otherwise
noted, the author and the publisher make no explicit
guarantees as to the accuracy of the information contained
in this book and in some cases, names of people and
places have been altered to protect their privacy.
Archway Publishing books may be ordered
through booksellers or by contacting:

Archway Publishing
1663 Liberty Drive
Bloomington, IN 47403
www.archwaypublishing.com
1 (888) 242-5904

Because of the dynamic nature of the Internet, any web
addresses or links contained in this book may have changed
since publication and may no longer be valid. The views
expressed in this work are solely those of the author and do
not necessarily reflect the views of the publisher, and the
publisher hereby disclaims any responsibility for them.

Any people depicted in stock imagery provided
by Getty Images are models, and such images are
being used for illustrative purposes only.
Certain stock imagery © Getty Images.

ISBN: 978-1-4808-7341-4 (sc)
ISBN: 978-1-4808-7342-1 (hc)
ISBN: 978-1-4808-7340-7 (e)

Library of Congress Control Number: 2019900455

Print information available on the last page.

Archway Publishing rev. date: 01/15/2019

Dedication

I would like to dedicate this book to Megan Davies, senior vice president at Lee, Hecht, Harrison, the outplacement firm contracted by my previous employer. Megan was my outplacement counselor. As I state in the book, Megan is a superb professional who helped me to realize that I was stuck in a rut, angry at my employer, and not moving forward to find a new position. She knew that on day 1.

She allowed me to take some time to get over the negative feelings I had, but she made me own my decision, my plan, and my outcome from our first meeting. That was the expectation, and we started from there. She was totally upbeat, and she treated me with respect and courtesy. She explained in detail the program, the resources, and how the office worked. Then it was up to me to decide how to proceed.

Megan was a professional in an industry focused on preparing you to find the right position. She had great ideas, contagious enthusiasm, and a very genuine way with people, and she made you feel like you were the most important person with whom she was working.

I know she was "just" doing her job, but she had an incredibly high standard and work ethic, and it showed. She absolutely wanted every client she worked with to be successful. She went beyond expectations every day to make sure that happened. I was very fortunate to work with her. She made a difference.

Lee Hecht Harrison had lots of great resources. I got great leads every day. I knew about all jobs available as soon as they were discovered on the many websites that LHH monitors. Remember this is what they do. With help from Megan and LHH seminars and resources, I decided to write this book and take a different life course. It was the right decision for me.

You see, I had this opportunity.

Contents

Preface

This is a little book, easily read in a single sit-ting if you are interested. But I would not suggest reading it in one sitting for most people who have just lost a job. Read until you have had enough— maybe an hour or a little more, maybe less, depending on how you react to the information. Then do something else before returning to it. You will get more out of it that way.

This is a book about a position lost, or a need for a change, and perhaps an opportunity found. This book is focused on middle and senior managers in large companies who have been terminated in some form or other. Sometimes it is called restructuring, downsizing, rightsizing or some other euphemism. It happens all the time. Some companies do it every two or three years. I hope the book will be of value to anyone who finds himself or herself unemployed unexpectedly.

It is about mourning the loss of the previous position and getting over it quickly and moving on to bigger and better things. It is also about using this event as an opportunity to evaluate your life position and your life direction. It is not a complete system, and it is only one tool. But it will get you started back up the mountain, to new adventures and better times.

I was a physician in private practice for twelve years. I had an opportunity to work with Senator John Heinz, our beloved senator from Pennsylvania who wanted to reform Medicare. Through this, I became interested in population management, using business "best practices" to develop programs to improve health of specialized populations of people. I made a decision to enter the business world, and I never looked back.

I became an administrator in a managed care plan and moved on to other business roles in health care with several different companies. Each position was better than the last, and I learned a lot about business. Each company had a culture, and I watched that culture change over time.

Business has changed a lot in the last twenty years. The average executive in a publicly traded business is with a company for three to five years, and this is dependent on the industry. For an individual who loses an executive position, it takes a while to replace a good position, and sometimes it does not happen. You have to make choices, and sometimes it is hard. There is no "best" solution in every case. But you do have options.

Nobody likes to be "job-eliminated." We all take pride in our work. But pride does not help replace that position with a better one. When I was terminated, I looked around for books and articles on how to get over the loss and move on. I found some things, but I did not find what I wanted or needed. So I worked to better understand what happened, why, and how. That is the basis for this book.

When I was in practice years ago, I wrote articles and self-help sheets for my patients. I even made self-help cassette tapes (that was the technology of the day) that proved to be very effective for some people.

They were short and sweet, and I was told that they helped a lot, especially in the acute painful time right after an event or loss, whether it was death of a loved one or loss of a job or illness, etc. They focused on a person's "self-talk," words and phrases used over and over that portray the emotions of the individual and reflect the present situation. Of course, I also followed these patients closely over time if they were having problems. Being a family doctor, I could keep track of how they were doing from other caring family members. We all have our self-talk, and we can change how we view a situation by changing the words and phrases we use every day. The concept of self-talk has been around for years, and the self-help industry has many resources that focus on self-talk. This book helps you to realize what you are saying and change it into a powerful force to promote your own well-being. This is one of several resources we will discuss in more detail.

When I first entered the business world, I found numerous books and articles on leadership and management that were very helpful in learning how to be a successful executive. Some of the best books were relatively short, very focused, and packed with practical stories and pearls of wisdom. I read them and passed them on to others. I hope my book will have that same practical wisdom and experience value.

I have been on a journey to deal with my own job loss, and it has been a positive adventure. I learned so much along the way. This book shares much of what I learned, and I hope it will be of value to you or to someone you care about who is experiencing an acute, unexpected job loss.

Getting through this can be difficult, especially if you have other stresses that precede the loss of your job. When you lose your job, you may lose your health insurance and financial stability. Many people try to "tough it out" without seeking help, even when help is definitely warranted. Every person is different, and every circumstance is unique, but there are some simple truths that can help. If you are anxious and/ or feel depressed or cannot sleep, you should see your doctor. This book is not a replacement for pro- fessional help that may be required for some people. The book points out several issues that may indicate when professional help should be considered.

This book focuses on you, and on getting you back into the mainstream again. Your comments and suggestions are appreciated. Positive comments are great, but critical comments are very much appreciated also, especially if you have suggestions for ways to improve the content and message. Visit my website, www.DrBobRobison.com, and use the contact form. There are several articles there that you may find helpful. I will be adding information as questions come up.

So you have this opportunity. Now, *get going again*!

—Bob

1

Why Are We Here?

The poet once said (also reported as the "Chinese curse"), "May you live in interesting times."

We live in interesting times. Information is all around, and disinformation abounds right along with it. You can find out so much about almost any subject just by using Google or Bing. If you are reading this book, I assume you lost your job, are losing your job, or want to leave your job. As you read, you will see statements in italics for emphasis. You will also realize that some concepts are repeated several times because they apply to the discussion at hand. This is purposeful. One of my more compulsive friends who previewed the manuscript highlighted all of the italicized phrases as he read through it. He was in a bad position and was contemplating a career change. He said the highlighted phrases helped him to make some changes in his thinking so that he felt ready to make the decision to leave.

Whether you like your job or not (and most of us like certain parts of our job and hate others), *leaving it causes anxiety.* Being laid off or having your job eliminated—or being outright fired—is painful. But it is not all bad. It is frightening to some and liberating to others, and how you respond is entirely up to you. In fact, *how you come out of this unexpected (and possibly unwanted) scenario is entirely up to you.*

I recently went through a job elimination. It came as a complete surprise. Things were going well as far as I knew. I had good reviews, and we were making money and improving the quality of our product and services. I had a meeting with my boss, and within the hour, I was out of the building, driving home with all of my stuff in a big box on the seat next to me—and I felt like a weight had been lifted off of my shoulders. I was surprised and a little numb. It was only later that I began to grieve for my old position, my colleagues, and my team, and I began to realize the loss that I was feeling. It was not anything that I did, and I was "eligible for rehire," as my boss related to me, but I still wondered whether there was anything that I should have done, could have done, or should not have done. My job elimination was part of a restructuring or downsizing. But it was difficult to accept. Doubt and grief are similar feelings, and they are additive in their negative effect.

In my years of medical practice, and later in the business world, I helped many people through the acute stress of losing a position. It was different then, and perhaps it was easier to get through. Back in the eighties and nineties, many businesses were family owned, and most of those were small operations by today's standards. Some businesses made it, and some did not. Layoffs occurred, and whole towns were adversely affected when the major employer had a layoff. But most people found work relatively quickly. Companies valued their workers, and workers were loyal to the company.

Big companies like Standard Oil and US Steel were around then, and unions provided a lot of protection for rank-and-file workers. But management has always worked at the pleasure of the owners. People worked for the same company for twenty or even fifty years sometimes, and at retirement, there was a pension that rewarded longevity.

Those days are over for almost all of us. Now we have the 401(k) and IRA rules, and we have frequent changes to the tax code, "bubbles" in the stock market, and more recently, the devastating and frustrating crash of the financial markets in 2007. Government employees and teachers may enjoy retirement plans, but most of us depend on our 401(k), IRA, and savings. And we control those funds—not the employer.

Our legislators really let us down in 2007. "Everyone" saw it coming, and regulations either were not adequate or were relaxed over time (that only prolonged the actual crash), but nobody seemed to be able to fix the problems until the actual crash happened. People warned about subprime mortgages several years before the crash, but lending was very competitive, and profits were a strong motive for continued bad behavior in the banking world. When it finally blew up, banks that were too big to fail were bailed out, and the whole world ended up in recession and depression. Funny how the banks came out of that bigger and stronger than ever. Looking back, we realized that there were many lessons to be learned. And we learned some of them but not all. That recession hit our retirement savings hard, and it took years to recover. We are only now able to look back and realize what happened and how it was resolved over time. People are not retiring at sixty-five if they are able to continue working.

In addition to this, we have an expectation today that we will live longer, and we have a fear that we could outlive our resources. Families are scattered over the country and over the world. The elderly fear infirmity and the financial drain it causes when they get cancer or have a heart attack. There is always a worry that our savings will not last, and we do not want to burden our children with our care in the future.

And now, thanks to restructuring, the position that you thought was secure is no more. Or that job of a lifetime is now a grueling nightmare. Same difference.

We often look to previous generations at times of stress. How did Mom and Dad and Grandma and

Grandpa get through these ups and downs? Frankly, they did not have these ups and downs. Life was simple, and the rules were simple compared to today. Multiple generations lived under the same roof. Families came together and everyone "took care of their own."

The truth is that the world has changed—and the rules have changed. Having a strong business ethic, a positive work ethic, and professional and personal integrity are not enough. In the past, the company founders cared about the product and their employees, and they built a solid company with a good reputation over multiple generations. The company had a commitment to its customers, and the company culture was good. Then they sold it to new owners with different business ideas. Or maybe they went public. The company culture changed.

That still happens today, but businesses today are often controlled by institutional investors and venture capitalists. Profit is their only motive for investing in a particular company. They couldn't care less about the product. Many times, they do not even know the product or how it is made and delivered to customers. But they know how much profit the company made last year. They compare their costs to their competitors. They are always looking for ways to improve the profit margin.

Some call it greed. Some call it the new normal. It is not good or bad, but it is different. The bigger the company, the more levels of management there are. People at the top make decisions that they should not be making. They do not understand the ramifications of their actions. Scorecards reflect profit—not quality and customer satisfaction. Big companies have no soul, and many have no mission beyond making a profit. I had a perceptive boss who told me that you could always understand confusing changes or decisions if you just followed the money. He was right.

That is why I wrote this book: to help you to understand what happened and get going again. We live in interesting times, and you can do everything right and still be out of work. Your perfect job can change over time, and you may not see the handwriting on the wall until it is too late. So now you have this opportunity to take stock of where you are, where you want to be, and what it all means. And you may be glad it happened—once it is over and you have attained your goal of finding a new and better position.

Some people call this a time of mourning and compare it to a grief reaction to the loss of a loved one. We like to think that we are much more than the job function we perform. But the truth is that people spend most of their waking hours either at work, thinking about work, preparing for work tomorrow, or worrying about some big project at work that will take all of their waking hours. Now, suddenly, there is no work to worry about.

It can be a negative and painful time, or it can be a positive opportunity to assess and reassess your goals, your life plan, and what you will do next. For many, it is a time of uncertainty and challenge. *You will stay in this place of uncertainty for as long as you wish, and when you are done, you will move on.* This is a time when family and friends can be helpful, if you allow them to help. It can also be a kind of "free fall," which is an experience that most of us would find a little frightening—and definitely not a positive time. But it is also like a vacation where you have nothing waiting for you when you get back and nobody calling you while you are trying to relax. The same glass of water is either half-full or half-empty, depending on how you look at it.

I was fortunate to have outplacement services provided by my employer. Many larger employers provide this benefit to their employees, especially employers who do this "not infrequently." My outplacement counselor, my guide to getting through this and finding a good position, was a down-to-earth, practical, experienced human resources professional at the outplacement company—and she was a positive person. She made a big impact on me. In fact, I dedicated this book to her. She got me going again. I do not think she treated me any differently from the other hundreds of clients that she has worked with over the years, but she calmly and patiently explained the services that her company offered and gave me a simple plan to start my process. I was angry and determined to feel sorry for myself, and she did not fight that, but she also did not honor that. There was an implicit expectation that she would only advise. I was free to accept or reject the services the company offered. *But I owned that*, not her. She smiled when she said it, but she meant it. She was just so nice about it. I needed that. I felt that I had been betrayed by the people I worked with every day. I needed a little understanding.

Outplacement services are very helpful. If your employer does not provide outplacement, you may want to consider working with an outplacement company at your expense. They have resources totally focused on preparing you to find potential positions that you may be interested in. Regardless of your abilities, experience, and industry contacts, a good outplacement company can offer you great resources. They follow many of the employers in a variety of fields. Good positions do not occur every day.

They review your resume, and LinkedIn profile, and give you meaningful input on content and style. Resumes are your first chance to make a good impression on a potential employer. They may be your last if you do not have the correct information in your resume in a professional, readable format. They give you a place to go on a regular basis to work on finding your next position. They offer information that may be of use if you are considering changing positions or industries. They offer training in various software programs and seminars appropriate to your job search. It took Megan an hour just to go over all the services her company offers.

That was my first "kick in the seat of the pants" to get moving again. It was a positive expectation that I wanted to move forward and that I would work to find a new position or perhaps change my life course and venture into another venue. (The sky is the limit when you suddenly have no obligations from the past.)

This was not just a process to find a new position to replace the one I lost. For me, this was a time to reflect on where I am, where I have been, and where I want to go. That is the opportunity to which the title refers.

When you are head down, nose to the grindstone, you are usually in problem-solving mode, fixing one thing before you move on to the next, waiting for someone else's poor planning to become an emergency, and working as hard as you can every day. All of a sudden, your life changes, and you have no fires to put out, no crisis to avoid, and nobody asking you to do the impossible. So *where are you, what are*

11

---

you, who are you, why are you, and where do you go from here?

This is the time of uncertainty, and also your time of opportunity.

You need someone to help you through this time of uncertainty. It can be a professional, a spouse, a friend, a recruiter, a psychologist, a pastor, a neighbor, or any combination of these. It may take a village in some cases. Maybe you can do it without help, but that is kind of like building a house without blueprints. It might not turn out as well as you hoped, or it might have problems with structural integrity. This is not rocket science, but it requires careful planning and effort. Experience makes it easier to traverse the path to success.

So this is a good time to adjust. You can change some things that perhaps are not working well for you. You may want additional training in Excel or Sequel. *Perhaps you want to reinvent yourself* in your industry or even change industries. But be wary of making big changes when you are feeling stressed. As the master carpenter said, "Measure twice, and cut once." You may want to measure six times, and even change the layout of the project. When you are confident that you made the right decision, it is easier to make it happen. We will discuss reinventing yourself later in the book.

If you are still mourning the loss, or if you are still angry, *take some time to figure that out.* You must figure it out! You can blame anyone you want, but it is entirely up to you to pick yourself up and decide what you want and where you are going. And when you are ready, you will move on.

And *don't take too long.* It will take time to work through all the things you need to consider, and the right job in the right industry may take a while to find. Days become weeks, and weeks become months, and your resume is going to show a hole that you will need to explain. Plus you will not feel relief until you have that next position or know where you are headed.

Read a book, watch a movie, or just take a short vacation. Why not? Doing something relaxing and different is a great stress reliever. Reflect on your present life situation and where you want to be. Do that project that you have been putting off. Wash the car, walk the dog, get some regular exercise, and smile. This book can help you with all of that.

Why do you need to understand what happened? It does not make a difference anyway. But it may help you to avoid walking into an even worse position next time. You decided to take this last job, thinking it was a good career move. Apparently, it was not, or you would not be unemployed and miserable. Everything that happens can provide some good learning. While you have the time, try to understand what you need to know from this experience to enable you to make a good decision about a new position, a new company, or a new career path. We will talk more about that later in the book.

When you have worked through your initial grief and anger, which can take from ten minutes to ten weeks or more, you are ready to move on. If you have not worked it through, or even if you have, events may happen that trigger a return to anger and grief. Understanding the situation will help you to get through those times quickly and effectively. This book will give you guidance.

2

The C Words

There are several important words that I would like to talk about, to help you to get moving, and they begin with the letter *C*. The words are: congruence, contradiction, conflict, change, and cognizance.

We will start with definitions, according to Merriam Webster, and Google Search.

Congruence: the quality or state of agreeing, coinciding. It is the harmony of daily life and an established routine. Congruence is wonderful in a person's life, especially as you get older and experience the normal ups and downs of life. When you are established in your adult life, moving through the ranks, getting promotions, obtaining recognition in your job and your career and your personal life, and improving your financial position, life is grand. You get up about the same time each morning, and you have a good idea from day to day what should happen, what will happen, and how that will give you advantage in the workplace and in your life plan. When the hammer comes down, and suddenly you have this significant change in your life and change in your daily routine and your career and your financial position, congruence becomes elusive. Life seems suddenly hard. Congruence is familiar and comfortable. Lack of congruence can be anxiety provoking.

Contradiction: a proposition, statement, or phrase that asserts or implies both the truth and falsity of something. It can also be a situation in which inherent factors, actions, or propositions are inconsistent or contrary to one another. Look at this recent change in life circumstance. *You certainly should not derive your sense of self-worth from your job.* After all, you are much more than just an employee of this company, and the fact that you are no longer employed by this company or no longer enjoying your work does not change that. So why do you feel so different now that you no longer are invested in that position?

Conflict: a competitive or opposing action of incompatibles; an antagonistic state or action (as of divergent ideas, interests, or persons, or a conflict of principles). Perhaps more appropriate for this discussion, conflict is a mental struggle resulting from incompatible or opposing needs, drives, wishes, or external or internal demands. As your previous congruence seems to melt away, you become aware of contradictions, and you see conflicts that were not important before. Most of the time, the conflicts are not new, but they may seem more important and pressing now.

Change: to make or become different. Change is a part of life, and one of the few constants in the universe. Change is always a part of life. But right now, some changes are welcome, and many are not. For most people, change is hard. But we adapt to change, and how quickly we adapt depends on many factors, especially age and health status. Some may be unique to your situation. Change is part of an active life. Dealing with change is a life skill that you develop over time. We call that flexibility (or lack of flexibility.) Change will happen whether you want it or not. *How you deal with change will affect your sense of well-being, and your success navigating through this unusual time.*

Cognizance: an awareness, a notice, or an acknowledgement. In this stressful moment, it is a developing self-awareness and sensitivity to the current situation and to the changes that are taking place. It is acknowledging and assimilating new information and new understanding of old information.

And there is one *D* word—*dissonance*—worth mentioning. Dissonance is a disharmony. It is in direct opposition to congruence. It is generally a negative process. *Dissonance is best described for this discussion as just static in the otherwise apparent harmony of life.* You must learn to see it, evaluate it, decrease it if possible, and many times just ignore it. Static is just noise. If it becomes more than just noise, take a moment to reevaluate it in light of your changing circumstance. It might be important, especially if it is frequent. Most static is just distracting and tension provoking.

3

Change: Opportunity or Challenge

Let's go back to the title of this book.

So you have this opportunity. You have a significant change in your life situation. Again, it could be an involuntary job loss. It could be a change in work circumstance such that your position now is untenable and/or uncomfortable to continue. It was not something you planned or chose to do, but it is here now.

For simplicity, let's stay with the example that your position was terminated. (There is a later chapter on the circumstance that you are still employed, but you are very dissatisfied with your position.) When your position is terminated, there is a change in your daily routine, because you do not have to go to work every morning. You may still get up at the same time, or you may stay up late at night and then sleep in the next morning. But you do not drive to work, and you do not have the next eight or more hours taken up with company business, and you do not have the drive home at night. You have free or unstructured time. You have time to relax and perhaps read a book or talk with friends. If you like to cook, or have a hobby, you now have time to enjoy pursuits that you did not have time for a month ago. You have time to fill. Enjoy it. If you do not do something constructive, you will be bored, and at the end of the day, you will not feel that you accomplished much. *This time void may affect your feelings of self-awareness and self-worth.* Free time can be challenging.

I am a board-certified family physician and was in private practice for twelve years. When I was in active practice, I had a psychologist colleague to whom I referred patients if I was not able to help them. He was a marvelous individual, very patient, and very wise. He had a few "golden" phrases that he used with patients, pearls of wisdom that were very helpful at times of stress. One of them was: "Stop trying to make sense out of nonsense." There is not always a logical reason for everything that happens. Even if you think you know the reason, how can you be sure? And why does it matter? It is done. Just accept it and move on. But how do you do this?

It is hard to accept something that makes no sense and causes such pain and loss. It is difficult to believe that karma just caught up to you or that nobody is to blame for the present circumstance. You could blame it on bad management or the corporate culture or just bad luck.

You have integrity. You take pride in the work that you do. There is pain now, and an acute sense of loss to be dealt with.

We believe that we are good people, and only good things should happen to us. (This does not mean that you did anything to deserve the bad circumstance you are now in.) We all know that bad things can happen to good people who did nothing to deserve the misfortune they now endure. And it does not even mean that what is coming is bad. It is a change, and change can be hard.

James Allen once said, "Circumstances do not make the man, they reveal him." James Allen was a pioneer in the self-help movement in England over a hundred years ago. This advice is timeless. *Regardless of why or how you got to this point, you now own it, and you need a plan to move forward from this point.* You own your destiny. How it turns out will depend on the decisions you make. These decisions and your resultant actions will show a lot about you.

So let us go back to the *C* words. A big *change* has occurred. You are not feeling the *congruence* that you used to depend on. There are apparent *contradictions* in life, and *conflicts* abound. This is perhaps your new normal, at least for the time being. This can seem like a free-fall situation, or it can feel like a new sense of freedom. The sky is the limit, or the walls are closing in, or maybe elements of both. Your glass is half-full or half-empty. But one thing you know for sure is that it is a big change. Embrace the change, and own your destiny. You need to move forward. You need a plan. So where are you, and *how do you begin?*

4

How Do You Begin?

Begin with the resources you have. Begin with you. What is your philosophy of life? We all have a philosophy. As a child and especially as a teenager, most of us thought we were invulnerable and immortal, at least for the immediate future. Do you remember taking chances then that you would not take today? As life progresses, with all its ups and downs, we realize that we have strengths and weaknesses, and that other people in our lives have an effect on our life's course and on our decisions. We see situations much differently than we did in the past.

With life experiences, we gain wisdom. With wisdom comes a broadening of our philosophy, a restructuring of our goals, and perhaps, at times, some adjustment(s) in those goals. What was important to us as children or young adults now has new dimensions.

Can you state your life philosophy in simple terms? How does it work for you overall? How is it working right now? Are you confident, doubtful, cautious, bold, arrogant, reserved, or apprehensive? At times of stress, we use our life philosophy to help us through the uncertainty and give us a road map to a more successful tomorrow.

I remember having life figured out at age twenty. I could tell anyone how to improve his or her life and his or her current situation. It seemed so easy. Just listen to me. Why can't you figure this out yourself?

At age thirty, with more life experiences, both positive and negative, I realized that some of my early ideas were probably too simplistic, and there were more considerations to be accounted for in making decisions on life direction and developing goals. One of the biggest changes in my life was having children. Prior to the birth of our first child, life seemed really simple and easy. Bringing a baby into the world now meant that we had this new person in our lives, and he was totally dependent on his parents for everything. Footloose and fancy-free days were now gone, replaced by the wonderful joys of parenthood, lack of sleep, and all that goes with it. I remember his first words, his first steps, watching him learn about his toes, and then slowly watching him grow up and test every rule in our family.

Suddenly, I was confronted with my need for short-term and long-term goals. The long-term goals were too big to handle, and breaking them down into short-term goals made them manageable. The devil is always in the detail. Now I had others to consider, not just myself. I had a wife, children, parents, friends, and colleagues who all had something to say or some need to ask for or some comment that was critical for me to hear and consider. I was becoming a responsible adult and hopefully growing into the role.

Did you ever meet a totally positive, always positive, sometimes unbearably positive individual? I have known several. They all had interesting stories to tell. They had hardships to overcome and problems to solve. And they solved them as they came up. They were not positive because their life had been perfect. They were positive because they had handled whatever life threw at them, and they felt confident that they could handle whatever came next. These are very interesting people to talk with. They are really inspirational. They can help you become more confident even if you are feeling less than positive overall. They usually do not advertise their life history or their problems. They just handle them.

Did you ever meet a totally negative person, always negative, sometimes unbearably negative? I have met several and treated some of them as their physician. These are people who seem to complain about everything and have no expectation that anything good will ever happen in their lives. Every day, they are confronted with painful situations, and they make poor choices with negative consequences. This type of person exaggerates the bad and discounts the good. These are people who can brighten up a room dramatically by leaving. These people can drain your emotional energy. You should interact with them in small increments if you can control that, especially during this time of transition. Negative people drain your emotional energy, especially when you are stressed.

These are two extremes, and most people fall somewhere between. They are, however, related. Most of us are very positive at times, but we can also be very negative at times. And it does not take something really terrible to transform a good day into a bad day. A stressful day can suddenly get much better when one good thing happens. You realize that things are not as bad as they seem. The value of having a simple, strong philosophy and a positive outlook on life is that it will help you to get through the difficult times, and it will make the good times even better.

It is easier said than done. Even the most positive people you know can have really bad days. Sometimes, they just hang on and wait for a situation to pass. Tomorrow is a new day. They know they do not have to confront every challenge immediately. Sometimes a situation can resolve or improve without their direct intervention. At other times, addressing a situation immediately keeps it from getting worse. They make an assessment and deal with issues as they are able. This is resilience.

How resilient you are in life situations depends on your emotional energy and your learned ability to handle issues. How you handle issues depends on your knowledge and experience. Resilience develops over time, with knowledge and experience. It strengthens your resolve to achieve your goals. It stimulates you to move forward and helps you to see the positive aspects of life. The challenge becomes an opportunity.

Most of the time, we respond to a feeling of sadness or happiness as much or more than we respond to the actual gravity or joy of a given situation. And here is the secret. If things have been going well, and you are getting a good night's sleep every night, eating right, getting exercise, and enjoying a period of low stress, you have more emotional energy to deal with the occasional curve-ball that you might encounter. *Situations may feel worse than they really are if you are tired or depressed.* You respond to the feeling rather than the severity of the situation.

Emotional energy is like the electrical energy stored in a battery. Chronic pain, whether physical or emotional, literally drains your emotional energy. You can recharge your battery and store up emotional energy, or you can drain it totally. You have to become aware of your emotional energy levels and make a conscious effort to conserve and even increase your emotional energy every day, especially in times of uncertainty. A restful night's sleep certainly helps.

Even the strongest person can have so much stress in a short period of time that he or she becomes negative and perhaps shows clinical signs of depression. But recognizing this, with the knowledge and ability to conserve emotional energy and rebuild energy stores, this person quickly gets back to a better state of mind. Are you aware of your emotional energy stores? Do you realize when you are becoming negative? Do you know what to do to increase your emotional energy?

Positive self-talk builds emotional energy stores. Negative self-talk drains emotional energy. We will talk about that later in the book, but for now, be aware that your emotional energy is not limitless. Learn how to conserve your emotional energy on stressful days, and how to separate the feeling from the actual situation. Every day is a new day.

Make sure your philosophy of life is simple, strong, and helpful to you. Know the difference between the gravity of an actual situation and the way that situation makes you feel. You cannot change the external situation, but you can do something about how you react to it. If you are getting down, do something to get positive again. Take a walk. Give someone a kind word or a compliment. Do something to change your daily routine. Call a friend or loved one and have a good conversation that will get your mind off of your situation.

Don't dwell on negative events like your job loss or other perceived "hurts." Every time you relive it, in total or in part, you use emotional energy to cope with the pain, the anger, the fear, and the doubt. Write down the issue and come back to it later, or talk with someone about it later. Try to handle bad news and stress in manageable increments rather than charging blindly into the night. Sitting in a corner reliving negative events just drains your emotional battery needlessly. If you think about something very stressful or negative for more than an hour, or talk for hours with your friends or even your counselor, recounting and reliving the painful details, you will be depressed and exhausted. You need to take a break before trying to address it further. Professional counselors limit sessions to an hour, or sometimes less. They know the consequences to the patient of dwelling too long on an issue.

I want to say something here about depression. If you are depressed, or have been prone to depression in the past, you may need professional help during this time of major life change. Dr. David Burns wrote a great book, "Feeling Good," which can help you understand more about depression and how to overcome it. There are many great books out there on depression, positive self-talk, and developing a great life philosophy. Here again, Google and Kindle and readily available resources are your friend. See your physician if you are depressed. Acute depression needs professional treatment. *If those who love you are worried about you, this is a good reason to seek professional help.* Drugs and alcohol do not help solve problems, but they can aggravate the negative feelings and cause you to become more depressed. This is common sense and simple wisdom.

This is a good time to address the issue of anger,

especially anger aimed at the person or persons that you perceive made the decision to eliminate your position or make your job miserable. Anger can be a useful emotion if it produces a change that helps you to move on. If you are in a competition, and a competitor has just bested your efforts, anger can push you to try harder and win. Anger can also be a bitter, repetitive energy waster. You are either in a bad job situation or you have been terminated (or why would you be reading this book?). If you can use your anger to motivate you to try harder to find the next wonderful position, then it may help you. But be wary of continued anger. It sneaks up on you, and it can totally drain your energy. You may begin to discount the many good things in your day because you are consumed with anger and a desire for revenge. Revenge is rarely a good thing. It never turns out as well as you would hope. And anger can push you to hurt someone badly. If you do, you cannot take it back. "Sorry, I was just so angry" does not help the person you hurt.

You really want to rise above any anger or petty revenge motives. Don't let anyone else have power over you in this manner. Most of us have inner mechanisms that keep us from hurting other people badly in revenge. We do not want to stoop to their level, even if we absolutely know they purposely harmed us.

I recently read a book entitled *Five Types of People Who Can Ruin Your Life*. The author, Bill Eddy, is an LCSW and attorney. LCSW is a licensed clinical social worker, a counselor who treats people with a wide variety of mental issues, including personality disorders. Mr. Eddy also deals with people with personality disorders in his work as an attorney. He describes a type of person who has a high-conflict personality, and may have one of several severe personality disorders. These people actually target others that they feel threatened by.

Where the normal individual might just dislike someone, a person with high-conflict personality views that person as a threat and focuses on how to take him or her out. These people know no bounds, and they may be clever enough to harm you in a way that you know it was them, but nobody else does. They take pride in that. I have known several people like that. If the person you are angry with is a high-conflict person, you may try to take revenge, and he or she will escalate his or her response to harm you terribly. Better to just move on to the next life challenge and be done with persons like that. These people are scary. They do not play by the rules that most of us live by. They do not even know what those rules are.

Back to your situation, remember that there is no way to go back and undo what is done. And there is no reason to. There are other positions out there, and you have talents and abilities that will allow you to find something better. This is your opportunity. Take it. *Leave the anger behind.* This is important. Yes, it is.

5

The Difference between Static and Disaster

Take stock of your present situation. Give yourself an afternoon or a day to think, assess, ponder, learn, and plan. Allow yourself more time to contemplate your options. It might take all afternoon or all month. There may be external considerations that will affect your ability to follow the course you want to take. Considering all the angles of a plan may cause you to change that plan or even discard it in favor of Plan B.

Do you have loved ones that depend on you? Do your parents need you, or will they need you more in the future, as they age? Do you have children who desperately want to remain in the same school situation, or with their friends? How would a move to another city or state affect them? How would it affect you?

Does your spouse have a really good position? If you are forced to move, will your spouse be willing to move? Do you want to consider another related or nonrelated industry? How much do you know about this new direction? How can you find out more? Do you want to go into business for yourself?

There are so many questions to consider, and some are more urgent than others. Some are more important than others. Some are vital and absolutely essential. Urgent is different than important. You need to look at both. Again, in the end, you will own the decisions you make, and the plan you develop. You have to get organized.

Get a notebook or a legal pad and start taking notes. Or set up a folder on your computer. *This is the start of your plan.* (See the illustration in the "Resources" section at the back of this book.) Keep it simple, direct, and focused.

Write down your thoughts, organize them, and discuss them with the significant people in your life who will be affected by the decisions you make. Start to plan, and write down enough comments about your plan that it begins to have a clear form. Usually a plan starts to take shape quickly, and each day brings new questions or new decisions. Once you start, you will find so many good ideas.

This is your part of the equation: the part you control—your ideas, values, goals, and how to put them all together. Life has some external factors that are beyond your control, and you need to understand these external factors and how they will affect your decisions. Maybe you need more than one plan, especially if you are considering multiple options.

Take a few days to go from a simple plan to a more comprehensive plan. Figure out the positives, the negatives, the timing, and the costs. And remember that you can change the plan to improve the outcome at any time. It is your plan. You can have multiple options, and the options you choose may depend on circumstances outside your control. And if an opportunity comes along that is not in your plan, consider how that opportunity would fit in with your priorities and the options you have already identified.

There is no magic outline or formula. If you are having problems, there are ready resources available on evaluating life options and goal setting. Search the internet or visit your local bookstore.

Here is where you need to really focus. Remember the word *dissonance*. There is always dissonance in your life. But if you are rolling along, you may not really be aware of the dissonance. It just does not bother you that much. I like to refer to dissonance as "static." It makes it seem inconsequential, and it really is. Static is just something that happens. It comes and goes, and it really does not have a significant effect on you or your plans for the future.

What is the difference between "dissonance" and "disaster?" Sometimes the only difference is your reaction. If something adverse happens, like your car won't start or you fall and break your leg, your reaction to the event or problem will determine if it is static or the end of the world. Most of the adverse issues you will face will be static and not disaster. You spilled coffee on your favorite shirt or blouse. That is not the end of the world. Yes, you may have to change your shirt or your entire outfit, and it may take a few extra minutes. So just do it and move on.

Get on with it. You have things to do. Don't worry about the small issues. Don't get distracted by them. And don't let small issues become magnified into larger issues. Maintain your perspective. Evaluate the significance of an issue and deal with it. Reevaluate it if something changes. Do not allow static to become a plan stopper.

Is it static, or a warning alert that something is not quite right, or is this an indication of a critical consequence that needs to be evaluated and understood and addressed in your plan? You can easily figure this out as you study your options and possibilities in an organized manner.

We all have an internal self-talk. It may not be an audible discussion. But it is there, and most of us are aware of certain expressions that help us to bring context to issues and events. "No problem" or "not a big deal" are two common examples of healthy self-talk. "Oh, no" and "Not Again!" are examples of negative self-talk that magnify the static into more of a disaster. The same glass can be half-full or half-empty, but you respond differently to a half-empty assessment than you do to a half-full assessment. Remember James Allen. Circumstances do not make a person great or small. They only reveal the strengths or weaknesses already inside of that person.

The great and simple truth here is that you can change your self-talk. It takes conscious effort. You may need others around you to help identify your negative thoughts. These may just be so familiar that you do not notice, but others close to you probably do notice. They see how the negative thoughts affect you, especially at times like this. You have to get rid of negative self-talk. Be diligent about it. You cannot afford the luxury of overreacting to static. You need to focus on the plan, and that leads us to Chapter 6.

6

It Does Not Matter

If you are thinking about leaving a terrible job, but you are not leaving it, there is a reason. There may be more than one, but there usually are only one or two major reasons. The real reasons may not be apparent, but start with the reasons that are apparent to you right now. If you already left the job, either voluntarily or, more often, involuntarily and with no warning, you need this same exercise.

Write down the reasons you did not leave the job or the things that concern you most about being terminated. Write one reason on each line, and skip one or two lines between. If you are out of work, write down all the important issues and feelings that are apparent to you right now, again skipping one or two lines between each issue. This is a very similar exercise in either setting. Let's start with some of the more common issues.

I cannot afford to be out of work.

It is not fair.

I did a good job, and they rewarded me with more stress, more work, and more problems.

It is not fair.

How will I support my family?

Why did this happen to me?

What will people think?

How will I find a job that can reproduce my current income, status, and potential for success in my career path?

It is not fair.

Okay, that is a good start. Maybe you do not identify with all of these, or maybe you have your own list. Now write each of your chosen reasons, one per line, and then after each of them, put down whether that matters to you at this point, either yes or no. Then put down why it matters to you, if it does.

Now cross out all the reasons that you put down, one at a time, and write the following phrase: "It does not matter."

Read over your list aloud, and emphasize the phrase "It does not matter." Say it several times, and say it out loud. It is important.

At this point, you may be ready to scream that it *does* matter, especially the one about supporting yourself and/or your family. How can some stranger in a little book tell you what matters?

Here is the important part of this discussion. We want to answer all of these questions with real answers that are relevant to you and your situation. But thinking about them, and using them as a wall to prevent you from moving forward *does not matter right now.*

What matters right now is having a plan to move forward. The clock is ticking. But before we leave these reasons that are of no consequence in forming a plan, we should have an answer for each of them, because they will keep coming up, and you have to get over this hump. It is static. Yes, as hard as it may be to hear this, it is static. It is distracting. It takes your energy.

So here goes:

- *I cannot afford to be out of work.* So what is your plan? You need a plan to get back into the game.

- *It is not fair.* Life is not fair. Life is not unfair. Fairness is a concept that is very important to most people. But it does not help you to get out of this problem. And if you come out of this time with happiness and wholeness, and most people do, this episode will not look unfair at all.

- *I did a good job, and they rewarded me with more stress, more work, and more problems.* Welcome to the current business environment. Perhaps you are not in the right position or even the right company. So remember to look for signs that your next position will not have the same issues, if you can. If you work for a company that you are not proud to work for, or a company that has no heart and no integrity, you will not be happy, and will not feel fulfilled. Finding a position where you feel you are contributing and where you feel valued is quite a blessing, if you can find it, especially in today's business world. You can work for a paycheck for a while, but unhappiness in your work is a terrible thing to deal with each day.

- *It is not fair.* We talked about this already.

- *How will I support my family?* This is often a show-stopper. The truth is that you may have to make changes, and they may be big changes. You need a plan, so that you can support your family. This cannot be a show-stopper. This is the entire show. You will need to take some time to plan away from the worst-case scenario. And you will.

- *Why did this happen to me?* Sorry, but this one really does not matter right now. It is important to look back and learn if you can, but it is not important right now. Maybe you made someone angry, or maybe you just were not a good fit. Or maybe this had nothing to do with you. Maybe it was karma or bad luck or just co-incidence. Don't let this stop you from making a plan and moving on. It may be worth looking back at this question after you have obtained your new, better position. And it may look very different at that time. There will be learning here, but only after you gain perspective and obtain your sense of congruence again.

• *What will people think?* The truth here is that *People will think what you tell them to think.* If you show maturity and wisdom, they will think that you are mature and wise and that you were dealt a bad hand. It happens to all of us. If you act crazy and become depressed, they will think you need help, and they might be right. Your self-talk will make a big differ-ence here. When an acquaintance asks, "How are you," they are really just saying "Hello." If you tell them you are very depressed, and not sleeping, and so angry that you cannot think straight, they will probably head quickly for the door, overwhelmed and not sure what to say but definitely wanting out of the room. *Tell anyone who asks that you are doing well, taking time to assess your options, and planning your next adventure.* This will become part of your healthy self-talk, and it will be true if you let it. Avoid the impulse to add the phrase, "under the circumstances." That little addition just signifies that you have not yet dealt with the issues. For the few people in your life that you consider significant, you can go into more depth. They are concerned about you and really want to know how you are. But even then, it is important to tell them that you are doing well and that you are planning and working your way through the issues to a better tomorrow.

• *How will I find a job that can reproduce my current income, status and potential for success in my career path?* You need a plan. *You may not be able to reproduce your current income, status, and potential for success immediately.* Your plan will include considerations of all of this. And your initial plan may change as you proceed with it. The job you find may be only a short-term stopgap, but it gets you out of a very stressful situation. That is still a positive.

- *It is not fair.* Okay; you have to give this one up! It is hard but so necessary.

As you go through this exercise, and perhaps when some of these ideas return at times, challenge yourself. Does this really matter? Why does it matter? If you are not sure, it probably does not matter. If it does matter, how can you best handle it?

Here is one last related issue. When your position is terminated, you may be inclined to look around and see who else was terminated. Were you the victim of discrimination? If you are over fifty, you may feel it was age discrimination. If you are a member of a minority, or identify as a certain race or ethnicity, or if you are LGBTQ, and you see others who were terminated who may be in a minority or a protected class, you may feel very strongly that you were a victim of discrimination.

Discrimination occurs in the business world. It takes many forms, and it is illegal in many cases. But it still occurs. Companies, especially large companies, have policies and procedures to prevent discrimination. It is difficult to prove that a company discriminated against a class of individuals. People have biases. Most people will treat you fairly, but one in ten may not, and some of those people are in management. If your manager does not like you for any reason, you may be vulnerable during a layoff. But is that illegal discrimination?

You may decide to take legal action at some point in the future. But consider your present situation. You could investigate filing an EEOC (Equal Employment Opportunity Commission) complaint. You can find out online what that means and what it entails. The EEOC will investigate the facts and make a decision. You will have to tell your story multiple times, and it will be stressful. Your employer may get a nasty attorney who will infer that you were not a good employee or that you could not do your job. They may investigate your past, and they could paint a picture of you that is not flattering. If you have a good case, you may get some satisfaction, but there will be a price to pay. It will add to your stress.

Even if the EEOC does not find in your favor, you can still file a lawsuit if you have a basis for the suit. Again, this is your decision to make. Discrimination lawsuits are long and drawn out. They are very stressful. Filing a suit and following through on it may be very expensive. Will a new employer want to hire you if you are suing your last employer? Should you disclose this information if you are contemplating a suit, or if you have filed one? Do you have the energy (and money) to go down this path right now? For many people, the answer is no.

The other side of this decision is that the company made a decision to terminate your position. Even if they reinstate you, would you want to work there again? There are books and online articles from people who have sued their employers that may give you valuable insights.

Don't let this distract you from your immediate goal. What matters now is finding a new position, a better position, and the best position for you. The choice is yours. Seek wise counsel from your family and friends if you are not sure what to do. The plan and the decision will be yours.

Now on to the plan!

The next chapter is for people who are still in the terrible job that they want to leave. If that is not you, feel free to skip to Chapter 8. But you may find some wisdom in Chapter 7, and remember that the job that you no longer have was not the ideal position you thought it would be. There is learning here.

7

Are You Still Here?

This chapter is for people who are in a bad job position, either because of internal or external circumstances. Many businesses today are public corporations. They are owned by institutional investors, venture capitalists, or both. The traditional "family business" is becoming rare. It was guided by the personal and family values of the founder(s), and these values were sacred. These core values helped to make the business successful. Almost always, quality was a key value. The customer was the focus. Profit was important, but as a consequence of running a good business, not as the primary motivation or short-term goal. Employees were considered valuable partners in producing the best products or services possible.

As control passed to the next generation, usually a son or daughter, the values and virtues of the first generation continued, and hopefully there was congruence across the business. Finances were always important, but the mission of the founders provided insight on how to solve problems and how to value service and business integrity. *Many entrepreneurs and small-business owners prefer working with smaller businesses that are not publicly traded, especially when they are purchasing services, because they feel the focus on service and integrity is much better.*

Large companies with multiple divisions may have multiple product and service lines, and sometimes these will conflict. The CEO has the responsibility to steer the course for the company, but the board of directors may feel the need for profit outweighs the traditional values of the company founders. In fact, institutional investors are looking for return on capital investment *only*. The venture capitalist is looking for leverage. When is this good business, and when is it just plain greed?

The balance between profit and quality changes.

Many companies fail with this kind of culture. But big businesses can weather the normal challenges of the economy and the market better than smaller concerns. Business good will is an abstract concept at best and is only important if the business is growing and giving good financial returns. The CFO becomes more powerful as the profit motive overcomes all other inputs. The tenor of management meetings changes.

If we lower the service level by 1 percent, our sales will not be affected, but we may save a few thousand to the bottom line. So we get a few complainers. The people promoting the change justify it by saying that it is not a big deal. Remember General Motors, General Electric, and all of the dot-coms. They found out the hard way that this may not be the road to success. But it took a while, and many people were affected before things went downhill.

The shareholder owners often do not even know what the company does or what products it makes or services it performs. They just know the share price, and the CEO is only as good as last year's results. In some cases, the entire management team is only as good as last month's results. The CFO may not even realize how the company operates or what the line staff does. The CFO uses "generally accepted accounting principles" to report performance and earnings. Scorecards measure only what senior management wants to measure. If performance suffers, the board will replace the entire management team.

When a company is bought, or when a merger produces big shake-ups in personnel, organizational structure, and direction, the changes can be monumental. Some may be good, as more resources are made available. But inevitably, the major value of the bottom line pervades every aspect of the company, and quality and integrity are just slogans. This can be hard to watch, and discontent may be palpable but unspoken across the company.

Here is a scenario that we have all seen time and time again in the business world. If there are ten people in a department doing a great job, and the staffing plan says that you need ten for the workload, why are we not replacing a person who left for another position in the company? The CFO or CEO will not approve the backfill. The board is pushing for more profit. Maybe it is year-end, and there is a hiring freeze. So the position is not replaced. Somehow the work gets done, as the remaining staff and perhaps the management staff in that department all step up to the challenge.

Then another person leaves, and now the remaining eight really have to work harder, and they feel the stress. Another person leaves because of the stress, and the CFO asks why we want to replace any of those lost positions, because the work is still getting done. (But the CFO seems to justify replacing the people in the finance department, because they all need to be there to get the job done. The CFO understands the finance department part of the business but not the actual service or product being produced.)

The business goes on, and the department is showing signs of strain. This department is in trouble. People are grumbling and complaining. But it gets worse. In fact, there is a new reorganization coming, and we now need to lay off two of the remaining seven people. But the reorganization will redistribute the work differently, and this will help. (Funny how that does not always work out as it was promised.) When we get down to five, and the employee satisfaction survey notes a loss of faith in management in that department, the manager is told that this is his or her responsibility to fix, and he or she better get morale to improve or else. This is a conundrum. The manager knows exactly what happened, but nobody above his or her level wants to hear it.

The stresses build, and profits go down. Is it bad management? At what level? The CEO and the CFO take no accountability, even though their lack of understanding of the business process was the ultimate cause of some bad decisions in retrospect. But the department manager gets the blame, and if that is you, nobody remembers or cares that you begged for more staff and told them this would be the inevitable outcome.

The situation blows up, and eventually the company is forced to hire additional people and get them trained, and now there is agreement that we really need ten people to do the work in this department. (Funny how that works.) New people need time to learn the job. Hopefully they are quick learners, and things get better over the next few months. But a lot of important momentum has been lost, and it will take time to make it work. There was no gain in this process. It was a bad decision made by people who just did not know.

But the manager and perhaps the director above the manager are gone. They may have been removed because of the poor performance of the department, or they may have left for a better work environment. Overall the company has suffered loss, but there is no scorecard designed to measure this. The CFO has no insight, and the CEO blames it on the manager and director. This is the way of the business world today.

In this scenario, nobody saw that the problem was not enough people. Actually, the people in that department saw that they needed more people. The staffing model showed that ten people were needed. The department manager also saw it, and warned of the consequences of the poor business decisions being made. The department kept trying to do more with less, and for a short period, things were okay. But it was not sustainable. How could this happen?

Does this sound familiar? Are you being asked to do more with less? Can you do the good job that you used to take pride in? Can you obtain more help? The CFO is not your enemy, but he or she is not your friend here. The CFO is always looking for ways to cut costs, and personnel costs are a major part of any corporation budget. The same issues apply to new or replacement systems, upgrades, and support services.

The real problem is that *people making these monumental decisions are not close enough to the actual work being done.* There could be five (or ten) layers of management, and people way up the ladder are making decisions that adversely affect all levels below them. They look at numbers, not people. The company is losing direction and losing its heart. A good staffing model is important to the success of the company, especially in service industries, but the finance and operations people often ignore the staffing model, except in their own areas of responsibility. They fail to realize that a 1 percent decrease in staffing may cause a 10 percent decrease in job performance in key areas, and once morale goes down, it is very difficult to get it back. Disgruntled employees may "retire in place," meaning that they do what they have to do, and start looking for a better place to work. They do not get involved when they see something that could be fixed or improved. They just lose interest, and it is difficult to see sometimes, especially for a busy manager who is short-staffed, overworked, and blamed for failure that is beyond his or her control.

Peter Drucker is often called the father of modern management. He believed that company management should value the employees of that company. While believing in the profit motive—and process efficiency and effective reporting—he also believed in the value of people. In his famous book *The Practice of Management*, published in 1954, he said,

> People as assets must be valued, measured, and developed. People are not hard assets that depreciate in value and can be written off; they are dynamic assets that increase in value with time.

If you are not valued, and only you can decide that, you should make a change. Perhaps you are not in the right position. Perhaps you are not in the right company. Perhaps you need to change both. You will make a change, or a change will happen anyway, *because your present situation cannot continue.*

Making a decision to not make a decision is basically making the wrong decision. Stated more simply: avoiding the decision is a bad decision with direct negative consequences.

There are consequences to remaining in a terrible work situation. It could adversely affect your health. Stress, burn-out, family conflict, and loss of effectiveness are inevitable if the situation is so severe. A heart attack is something that nobody should have to go through because of their job.

So you need a plan. You need to improve your current working conditions, or you need to find a new place to work. To quote Mr. Drucker again,

> Plans are only good intentions unless they immediately degenerate into hard work.

Is your current life at work enjoyable, miserable, or

some of both? If it is miserable, and you do not see that this will improve, you really need a plan. How bad is it? If parts of it are miserable, is this a temporary situation? Can you improve your job situation? What can you do?

Leaving can be an opportunity. It may be a last resort. It may be both. Only you can decide. And only you can make a plan to improve your situation. And remember, it has to be a good plan. You will own it.

Start it now. It will take a while to complete and execute.

8

Planning

There are many different ways to plan. Some people are very good at planning. Most people are not, or they just do not take the time. You will need three things to be able to say you actually have a plan.

The first thing you need is an accurate assessment of your current situation, your assets and liabilities, and your short-term and long-term goals. If you are still in your position, what will your company say if they find out you are looking for another job? What will your boss say? Who can you trust? Who should you not trust?

A good rule of thumb is that most secrets do not remain secret for long. Business environments involve personal relationships, and it is amazing how many people may know you, or know of you through mutual friends and acquaintances. If you are looking to transfer to another position within the same parent company, many companies have rules that you have to notify your boss. Find out what those rules are, and make sure you follow the rules. There may be risk if your boss finds out you want to leave, even if you are following the company rules. If you do not follow the rules, you may not be allowed to leave, or you may be terminated for not following the rules.

If you are no longer with the company, how will you find out about available positions? How will you decide what direction you want to take? Do you want a similar position, or do you want to adjust or change your career path? Do you want more responsibility or less? This is where the opportunity lies.

Here comes the hard part. What is the current environment in the industry for positions that you are focused on as potential opportunities? There are so many job boards, and larger companies have multiple postings in your local area, and perhaps across the country or across the world. You will have some work to do here.

What does your family think about a possible move? Do you have children or elderly parents, or other responsibilities that make relocation problematic? How much would it cost to relocate? Will a new employer pay for relocation at your level? Where in the country or where in the world would you like to go? Use all of this information to develop the outline of your plan. This will be your blueprint.

Now for the second part of the plan. What is your timeline? Do you want to move when the kids are out of school? Would you move first and then bring the family later? Realistically, how long do you think it would take to find a good position and actually make a move? How much longer can you tolerate your present circumstance? You do not need project management software to set up a timeline, but you should be realistic in your expectations. And you need a projected timeline as an organizational tool. Life is three-dimensional. Time is a fourth dimension of change and opportunity.

Who do you know who has made a move like you are contemplating? It may be time to take someone to lunch and see what you can learn from someone who successfully made a move. Did the person jump from the frying pan into the fire, or did he or she find relief from the unbearable stress of a bad job situation? We all know someone like this, and there are great books out there to help you with the planning. It is beyond the scope of this little primer to give you all the ins and outs. This book is just to get you started.

Remember that *it probably will take longer than you think to make this happen.* You have to plan a move, find a good position, and go through the interview process. And you may not get the first job you are interested in.

Now for the third part of the plan. Own it. You must own it. It makes a big difference.

There is no blame from here on. There is only accountability, and it is all yours. When you are successful, it will be because you, with your spouse or significant other, and perhaps your friends and your colleagues all worked together. If you own it, you control it. If you do not own it, then you may believe you are helpless to act to change it. Victims in this sense are people who find themselves in dark and dingy holes, and then complain because it is dark and dingy. The whole purpose of this book is to put the negative thoughts away and focus on obtaining a successful outcome. This is hard work, but owning the plan gives you the ability to make it happen, and when it happens, you will be so glad you did it. If you own it, you are not a victim, *and you can change the plan.*

Again, at any point, if your plan is not working, you own it, and you can change it. Change the goals, change the process, and change the outcome.

When you Google "finding a new job," Google returns 525 million results. Scanning down through the first fifty results; there are so many different types of entries. There are government jobs, recruitment companies, private companies, outplacement companies, and volunteer opportunities. Within your industry, there are probably several large companies, and many smaller companies that you can look at. You do not need to look at them all. Select a few entries that sound good, and spend some time thinking, dreaming, and planning. Do your homework. It is important. Without effort, your results will be less than optimal. Time spent here gives big returns.

Put in your search criteria. See what you get. Refine your search. Make it more specific. What qualifications do you have, and what qualifications or training do you need to move up to the next level? This takes time, and you need to take the time. Make some notes, and do not be afraid to change your plan. Think about your career goals. Career path is a concept that most people need to look at more frequently. There are immediate goals and long-term goals. If you want to become the CEO someday or move to the corporate level, you might need more financial knowledge and experience. Maybe you need to get a graduate degree in business or maybe more experience in other aspects of the business. What is the logical next step in your career process? Now is the time to initiate that path.

You can reinvent yourself and refocus your career goals at any point in this process. You will need a story to tell. You will need to get past initial screening of your resume, so make sure you have the key words. What does your LinkedIn say? Do you need to contact recruiters? Are recruiters contacting you?

There is so much more to planning, but much of it flows naturally once the momentum is established. Your plan can be simple or elaborate. *If you put more time into it, you will probably get more out of it.* Keep it as simple as you can and still have a plan that includes contingencies.

There is something to be said for luck in all of this. Maybe you will be fortunate enough to be at the right place at the right time. Maybe you will make your own luck by planning and making good contacts, and then when something good comes along, you will know it and be ready to go for it.

I believe that people learn patience as they move through a job search. It usually takes more time than you anticipate. If you are out of work, the financial pressures will build over time. Your plan needs to think about this also. How can you adjust your expenses so that you come through this period successfully? All of this is part of your plan. Hopefully, you have a financial planner, helping you to prepare for retirement. What are your options? Depending on your age, you may be able to borrow against your retirement funds or tap into investments. This should be part of your plan also, and will need to be revised at times.

9

Life and Finances

This will be a difficult discussion for some people. And *it will be a different discussion for younger people than for older people.* Adults should have a financial plan, and any life goal needs a plan to attain it that includes the costs involved.

Before you lost your position, hopefully you were in some kind of retirement savings program, whether an IRA, 401(k), pension plan, etc. Pension plans are not common anymore. They were great, because they did not involve a lot of decisions on your part. The employer put the money into the plan, either by defined contribution or defined benefit, and you got a statement at regular intervals telling you how much money you had, how much was vested, etc.

Most people who read this book will probably have

money in an IRA or a 401(k) plan, and not in a pension plan. Both of these require decisions on your part, and both have tax consequences. You may be able to borrow against your retirement savings and get a very low interest rate on the loan. But it is still a loan, and you have to pay it back. But you pay it to yourself, except for a small carrying charge from the company that supports the program. The bigger issue is that any money you borrow is no longer in your retirement program, and you are losing the increasing value that would accrue over time if it was invested. If you were earning 12 percent on the money, and you borrow it, you may be able to borrow at 4 percent, but that means you are losing 8 percent. However, if you had to take out a regular bank loan, you would probably pay a lot more than 4 percent annually in interest. There is no shortcut or rule of thumb to guide you. Get a calculator and a pencil and paper, and figure out all the costs and how it compares to other ways to obtain money.

If you are young, and have not been contributing to the retirement plan for long, you may not have much saved. And you probably can only borrow 50 percent or less of the vested amount. And you have no way presently to pay it back, so that could be a problem. But if you have the ability to borrow against your retirement plan, you may have a source of funds that you can use in an emergency.

Details and decisions beyond this point should be discussed with your financial planner or someone in your circle with financial knowledge and experience that you really trust. And be prepared for two different opinions if you ask two different people the same question. Everyone has his or her favorite way of handling retirement dollars. Some financial planners will counsel you to avoid home equity loans, and never borrow against your 401(k). If you have equity in your home, you may have a source of immediate cash, but again, you will have to pay it back, and you must plan for that. One more point, when you are terminated or leave the company for any reason, you no longer can borrow against your 401(k) in most plans, and any loans outstanding may become due and payable. Again, check out the details before you decide.

Here is the hardest part of this chapter. *How can you cut back on your expenses with minimal effects on your lifestyle?* Most of us spend more than we absolutely have to. We use our money to obtain a variety of things that we desire. Eating out is a necessary expense when you are working sixty hours per week. But it might save you a lot of money to eat at home if you are unemployed. Some people cancel their Amazon Prime and cut up most of their credit cards to avoid the temptation to buy, buy, buy.

There is a difference between being broke and being poor. Being broke is a temporary condition. Being poor is also a condition, but more importantly, *it is an attitude.* If your self-talk turns to, "I am just so poor," you may become poor in spirit as well as poor financially. I refuse to be poor. I am actually rich beyond measure. Every day is a gift, and every person is a joy to meet and interact with. I will never be poor, even if I am broke and have been broke for a long time. I refuse to be poor.

Compare your condition to someone that you know who has had a severe life adversity. When a person develops cancer, that person may need specialized treatments that are either not covered by insurance or are only partially covered. It is a shame that health insurance is not comprehensive, especially for cancer, and the longer it goes on, the worse the financial condition becomes. A severe chronic illness—whether cancer, heart disease, progressive lung disease, or other condition—may cause a person to lose or leave their job. Sometimes the person may become eligible for Medicaid, but Medicaid benefits depend on the political party in power at the time, and benefits can change quickly. A severe traffic accident can have similar consequences to chronic illness.

Compared to that kind of pressure and pain, your situation does not look nearly as bad. You have your good health. You have a temporary circumstance, and you need to take some steps. You need to take stock of your current situation and decide how much you can change it and how quickly you need to change it. *Remember that broke is a temporary condition, and poor is an attitude.*

Unless you are incredibly lucky, and very few of us are that lucky, planning is the best way to obtain a better outcome. Planning is solid. Luck is fickle. A budget will help you to plan. Following a budget may be difficult, especially if you really get tight with your money. But making the changes that will give you the best savings, with the least change in lifestyle and daily routine, will give you the most satisfaction. Cooking at home can be simple, and may even give you great joy and a sense of accomplishment. It will also fill your day with beneficial activity.

If you have a spouse and children to consider, then include their concerns as you develop your plan. They can help you to plan and to execute the plan and stay on track. Make it a game, to see who can do the best with sticking to the plan. When life gives you lemons, make lemonade. A supportive family is a real strength and comfort in stressful situations.

Be very honest with yourself and others, and update your plan as time continues. Some positions take several weeks to replace, but many will take more than four months, and very high-level positions are not that frequent. How much money do you require each month to stay current on your bills and obligations? Where will that money come from, and how long will you anticipate needing that before you find another position?

If you are contemplating leaving a position, you must consider what the potential loss of income will mean. It is far easier to obtain a new position when you are employed. You have more and better contacts on a daily basis. If you leave, you may have to join a new company at a lower position. How much of a decrease can you take? How much do you pay in taxes and other payments, for example, retirement contributions, stock plans, etc.? If you made $20,000 less in gross income, what difference would that be in cash in hand?

If you are under severe stress, you may decide to just quit, but that is unusual and should be avoided if possible. If you are in doubt, start accepting recruiter calls or call a recruiter that you trust and inquire about jobs in your area, and talk with colleagues at other companies. Always be aware that confidential is a relative term, and word will probably get back to your boss at some point. Be prepared for the discussion that may ensue.

This is hard, and a little scary to contemplate. Planning will give you a much better result, and it is possible to make a plan that will help you a lot.

Again, you own it, and you control it. And you have this opportunity to consider.

10

Nuts and Bolts

Next comes the nuts and bolts of this plan. Really good positions will have many applicants fighting to be hired. Managers do not have time to read every resume, and many companies use nonhuman screening methods to limit the candidate pool they search from. There are key words that these robot screeners look for. LinkedIn is commonly used by recruiters and HR professionals to find potential candidates. Read your LinkedIn information and polish it.

You need a resume that focuses on your talent, education, and experience, and tells anyone who reads it who you are and where you want to go. There are talented people who are very skilled at writing and editing resumes. They know the key words that need to be there. Unless this is your specialty, it might be worthwhile to get some professional help with this. There are different styles, and sometimes less is more in a resume. If someone is interested, they will ask you for more information. Having someone do your resume is not expensive in the long run.

You need to develop your story. If you get an interview, you will only have one chance to make that good first impression. Interviewers will ask you your strengths and your weaknesses. Expect a question where you are asked to discuss your weak points. How will you answer? There are strategies to guide your responses. Again, put some time in before any interview, so you know something about the company and can *show interviewers that you know a lot about the industry and about their company.* You never know how an interviewer may interpret your response. There are many good books and articles on resumes and interviewing. Your competition for the position will probably be reading this information and preparing for the interview. You must do the same, but do it better.

This is hard work and important work. But the next piece is absolutely critical.

Work on your attitude. Attitude is so important. A positive attitude is vital to your success. If you are out of work for several weeks, or months, it is difficult to maintain that attitude, but in many industries, the average time to land a solid new position can be three to six months. Your attitude may make the difference between being selected to move to the next level in the hiring process or being eliminated from the process.

Your physical health is also important to the plan. Gaining thirty pounds is never a good idea (unless you were underweight to start with.) But it can happen when your routine is disturbed. Losing a few pounds can be very positive for most of us. Improving your health and your level of physical fitness is great for your attitude. A new job will require you to put in "learning time," and this takes energy. If it is a good position with a lot of responsibility, you may be required to hit the ground running. There probably will be some problems to clean up from the last person who held that position. Get yourself ready. If you need training or need to learn new things for a career change, now is the time. Again, get yourself ready. This is all part of the plan.

11

How About Your Family and Friends?

For most of us, life is a family affair. We have a spouse or significant other person in our lives. We have parents and siblings. We have children. They may be dependent on us, or they may be on their own, but our success is very important to their success in many ways. And, of course, they are worried about us when life is stressful. They love us and respect us and worry about us.

Many years ago, when I was an intern working in the intensive care unit of a large hospital, I had to interact with a very close-knit family trying to deal with the patriarch of the family, who had just had a serious heart attack. He was lying in an intensive care bed close to death, and it was impossible to predict if he would last the night. The next few hours would be critical. He was in a coma and could not respond. As I entered the intensive care waiting room, I saw the family in one corner of the large room. I quietly observed them, wondering how each one was coping. I walked over to his wife and introduced myself. I would update the family when anything changed.

Mother was quiet, sorrowful, and obviously worried. She looked at her three children and seemed to worry more about them than about her husband. She told me that night, in a calm, quiet tone, that he had lived a full and wonderful life. He was sometimes impossible to live with, but he loved his wife and he loved his family, and he would do anything he could to support them. They had enjoyed a wonderful life together. He was not afraid to die, and she was not afraid to let him go. The alternative might be to watch him linger in a nursing home bed and die slowly over several months. She did not want that, and she was sure that he did not want that either. She was worried about how each of her children would cope with this situation.

The oldest son, Peter, was pensive and anxious at

times. He had just arrived from Chicago, where he worked as an investment broker. He had not been home in over a year. He paced across the intensive care waiting room. He talked about changes that would need to happen. He told his assembled family that Dad would never be the same. They needed to think about selling the house.

Peter stated that he would naturally assume control of the finances, and would make sure that everything was taken care of. He was the named executor in Dad's will. Mother reminded him gently that the will was very simple. Dad and Mom had matching wills that said that everything would go to the surviving spouse. Mom was not ready to even think about anything beyond that at this time. He was frustrated by that response. But he would not press the discussion any further. There was a lot of frustration and conflict bottled up inside of him. Why did this have to happen now?

The daughter, Joann, was sobbing hysterically. She blamed herself for not coming home more often. She wanted another chance to show her dad that she loved him. She felt like her father was going to be taken away from her, and she was helpless to do anything about it. She could not care less about Peter's rants and raves.

Tommy was only sixteen and was the only child still living at home. He fought with his father almost constantly. He wanted more freedom and more independence, and he was always broke. He had a loud discussion with his father earlier that day, and said some things that he was now very ashamed of. He respected his older brother, and they were very close. But he did not agree with Peter that they needed to sell the house or change anything in their daily lives at this point. He just wanted his father to get better.

I was concerned about this family. My heart went out to them. I wanted to help them. I wanted to say some very wise words that would comfort them and give them hope. Given Dad's condition, I really thought his demise was imminent. There was not much hope for improvement. They accepted me as the doctor spokesperson, and I gave them updates throughout the night.

I tried my best to explain in layman's terms what had happened. I felt that was my job, and I was trained to do that. Dad had a very small clot in the artery that went to the septum of the heart. That area generated the heartbeat, and the clot caused that natural generator (the pacemaker) to stop producing the electrical impulses, and his heart stopped. He passed out, and never regained consciousness. His heart responded to CPR, which was initiated immediately thanks to the quick actions of a volunteer firefighter who witnessed the event. The heart was beating regularly now, but the next twenty-four hours would be critical. And, of course, he needed to regain consciousness as a first step to recovery. They understood the situation.

I wanted to comfort Mom, but she was only focused on her family. I wanted to tell Peter to cool it, and I wanted to tell Joann that she was not to blame, and everything would be okay. But I did not. I had no way of knowing what the next day would bring. I did not want to add to their stress by saying the wrong thing. So I watched and waited with them.

Tommy seemed to be coping as best he could, and he and his mother talked quietly and reminisced about memorable moments in the past and how happy the family had been. The tension was palpable, but all was quiet for the moment.

I related all of my observations to the attending physician when he arrived. He had known this family for many years, and he knew each of them well. He asked me how I would handle each individual family member, especially if Dad did not survive the night. I gave him my observations and concerns, and he nodded. When I told him that I was afraid the family would fall apart, he seemed to smile just a little.

He told me that this family was doing very well and was coping as best they could with the uncertainty of the moment. Peter was being Peter. Peter was always Peter. And he would be fine. Joann needed to cry and express her thoughts. That was her coping method. She was very outspoken always. Tommy would need some care, and Mom would see to that. And Mom was an absolute rock. She would get over any obstacle that life put in her path. She was focused on her family, and that is where she wanted to be. She loved her husband dearly, but at this moment, her children needed her. Dad and Mom had always been a team. They had their moments. They had actually

separated at one time but came back together after some marriage counseling. They seemed much
closer after that episode. That was years ago and was
not relevant to the current situation.

In short, this family was doing fine, given the circumstances that had been thrust upon them. I was
relieved to hear that, but it took me a while to understand it and appreciate it.

I had many more episodes with families under stress
over the years, and each was different. I came to realize and respect the power and strength that a family has at times of acute stress. There are no magic
words of comfort. Being there is what is important.

Families in times of stress act just like they do in
times of joy and happiness. There are patterns that
are natural and normal and expected for them. If
these patterns are disturbed, that would be a cause
to worry. This family was doing fine and would do
fine through the crisis. Some of them might seem to
fall apart, and the rest of the family would come to
their aid. This was a family acting like a family. There
was respect and love evident in every interaction.

I transferred to a different service in the hospital the next day and did not see this family again. I did see the family physician again, and he told me that Dad never regained consciousness and died peacefully. Everyone (except me) thought I did a great job supporting the family through their crisis. I never did find the elusive words of wisdom that could make coping with something like this easier. But it was enough that they acknowledged the pain and reached out to each other in love. They had each other to lean on, and they all got through the very painful, acute loss of their husband and father over time in their own ways.

It taught me a valuable lesson. A functional family is a blessing in times of crisis. Stress produces some evidence of dysfunction in individuals within the family, but, overall, the family unit is a powerful force. Each member of this family team acted in a predictable manner, and each one drew strength from other members of the family.

If you have a functional family unit, you are blessed. Respect that family team, and use it for comfort and support. You can lean on them, and they will be there for you. You may be part of more than one team. If one or both of your parents are alive, you are part of that team. If you are married, with or without children, you are part of that team. If you are single or divorced, you have family, friends, a significant other person in your life, a sibling, a best friend, or perhaps a group of very special friends as your team.

These teams are not there to solve your problems. *They are there to support you* in any way that they can, and they believe in you. They do not assess blame. Their faith in you does not depend on your actual ability or experience. It is absolute faith, and absolute faith can give you great comfort and support. If you are hurting, so are they. If you are depressed, that is depressing to them. Each family member responds differently, but *they are all doing the best they can do. And so are you.*

Honor your spouse, your parents, your children, and your friends during this time. Enjoy the support that they can give you. Do not discount their ideas. Be sensitive to their concerns. They are trying to help you to figure out the plan, and they want the very best for you. If one of your family members asks how you are doing, usually that person wants to know that you are okay. They do not need a blow-by-blow description of the last seventy-two hours. If they want more, they will ask. If you are doing okay, just say that. If you feel the need to elaborate, do so. This is easy. This is family.

If you have a dysfunctional family, you probably already know the issues, and you have coping mechanisms. These mechanisms may be stretched during these stressful times, but they will work. You may have to look elsewhere for the support that you need at times. It is wise to stay close to family members who are functional and strong. They can and will help you to the extent that they can. It is also prudent to not be around the more dysfunctional members of the family any more than you have to. They can drain your batteries. With families, you may not have the luxury of picking your times to interact with each family member. Life happens, and you and they will do the best that you all can do.

Maybe you need a vacation or a few days to just get away from the stress and reconnect with your family and your world. It does not have to be a world cruise or a trip to Disneyland. But take time to decompress and reconnect with your family and friends and the supportive individuals in your life. Do it as often as you need to.

But perhaps you say you do not have time or money, and you are barely hanging on. Then perhaps you should read parts of this book again. The stresses are getting to you. Your coping skills are not working. It may be time to examine your plan, and see if you need to adjust or readjust parts of it. Where is your positive attitude? Where is your discernment? Where is your perspective? Maybe you need a vacation or a long weekend away to relax.

The glass of water is either half-full or half-empty. Decide that it is half-full. Keep it positive, and get rid of the negative self-talk that is threatening to overwhelm you. Let your family help you. Own your destiny. Own your plan. *Own your life.* What do you want to do?

12

A Word about Faith

Faith is believing in something, even when you cannot see it or prove its existence by any concrete terms. For many of us, faith is the belief in a higher being. It is a system of beliefs that explains our existence and gives us hope for the future.

Most of the great figures in history had a strong faith that sustained them in times of conflict. It also served to guide them in times of peace and, on more than one occasion, took them into times of conflict and crisis, for example Martin Luther King Jr., Joan of Arc, the disciples, etc.

Faith can make an important difference in our lives. At times of stress, when conflict challenges our self-esteem, and doubt threatens our feelings of self-worth, we find out just how strong our faith is.

Dr. Bob Robison

You have undoubtedly been through times of stress in the past, with the death of a loved one or a significant adverse event in your life. This time of job uncertainty is no different.

I wish for you a simple, strong, effective faith. I wish for you a faith that will sustain you and keep you whole in times of adversity. I wish for you a faith that gives you a sense of peace and congruence when life stresses seem to be growing each day.

Life is a series of ups and downs. It is a chain of challenges, each of which brings knowledge and wisdom as you overcome the obstacle. My mother used to say that growing old was not for sissies. Life can be hard, but living life successfully is beautiful. Life is beautiful. It can also be bittersweet at times. Faith helps you to make sense of life and gives you hope for tomorrow.

Can you put your faith into a few sentences? Can you relate to others how you are inspired and how that inspiration affects your reaction to the world? Great authors and poets have written volumes about life and faith. For those of us in the Christian religion, the Bible serves as an in-depth record of the trials of life and the power of God. Other faiths have their doctrines, and their history of life through the ages. Faith is important, and what or who you have faith in determines who you are and who you become.

I understand faith on a basic level. I understand prayer as a vehicle to communicate with God and to describe my concerns, and my ideas, and to receive understanding from God. My faith is simple. It works for me. I make mistakes every day. Luckily, I am not punished for my failings or rewarded for my accomplishments. Rather, I learn every day from my successes and my failures. It is easy to believe when you can see evidence of God, like when a true miracle happens before your eyes. It is more difficult to believe when you cannot see that evidence.

But when you believe and your faith is strong, you will see things that were not apparent before. Only when you believe can you see how it all fits together perfectly. You must believe before you can truly see. That is faith. Some people see coincidence. I see how seemingly unrelated events become a pattern that leads to greater happiness and success. Each religion is different, but certainly faith helps to sustain us in times of strife and discord.

I get great delight in helping others, especially persons who have no expectation that anyone will do anything good for them. I have been helped by others, and I absolutely endorse the concept of charity to others. I get a good feeling inside when I can help someone else just as others helped me along the way.

You cannot pay back the benefactor who helped you years ago. But each act of kindness gets magnified a hundred times when you incorporate new people into this chain of helping others. Whether it is a simple act of kindness or helping others in need on a larger context, I believe that your random acts of kindness to others come back to you as blessings in your own life. These are mostly strangers, not friends or relatives.

I may never pass this way again. I want to make the world a better place with little steps, many steps, in concert with others of like persuasion. I find joy in doing it. It does not have to be expensive. Sometimes just a smile or a kind word makes a big difference.

The church can be a wonderful place to renew your faith and to rebuild your energy. It can be a place to find strength and comfort. It can be a place of refuge, or a comfortable place for renewal. It can be a church, synagogue, temple, mosque, or any gathering of people of faith who want to make a positive difference in the world.

You can make a difference in the world in simple ways. When you get discouraged, and life seems dismal and foreboding, try smiling. Give someone who needs it a little boost or just a kind word. What comes back to you will inspire and empower you. It is simple, and you can do it every day. *Life is short. Enjoy every day and every hour.*

13

Reinventing Yourself

You can make changes in your life whenever you want. You do not have to wait for a crisis to look around and see what is happening in your life. Since change has now been forced upon you by outside forces, it might be a good time to look at who you are, and who you are known as. Change is coming already, so how can you make it better?

We all live in multiple spheres. We have family, friends, neighbors, colleagues in our company, and perhaps colleagues in our industry nationally. Some people actually have a global network. When your name is mentioned, an image comes to mind. People who know you remember how you looked when they saw you last. In the business community, people who have never met you may know an article you wrote or remember a phone conversation, or perhaps you coined a phrase, or maybe you sent a classic email that described the solution to a complex problem, and suddenly you became linked with that across the country.

Hopefully you are not known because of your droll disposition or your bad jokes or how you act or dress, but that is possible too. Those more casual and less representative characterizations are easy to dispel. They are based on poor-quality interaction, and the moment someone meets you, they will realize that you are a person of greater depth and great integrity and purpose. Or will they?

In the last six months as the stresses built, did you respond negatively to the stress and become less outgoing, more irritable, and even difficult to communicate with? Who are you, and how are you known today? Do your children like you and appreciate you? Does your spouse still enjoy your company, or does he or she try to limit the conversation to topics that will not set you off?

Are you still the same person that you used to be? Are you happy with who you are and who you have become? If not, change it. Change it now. This is part of the opportunity of your current life circumstance. Take a close, critical, hard look at yourself and how you are perceived.

There is a common wisdom that it takes thirty days to change a habit. That may be an average, and there may be studies to back it up, but there is no natural rule that says a habit can be changed in thirty days, and if you only work on it for fifteen days, it will surely come back. You become what you think about becoming.

First, take stock of who you are and what you might want to change. All changes produce outcomes. Are there any downsides to the changes you want to make? Look around you at persons who you admire, and ask yourself if they have certain traits that you should emulate or assimilate. Some changes are simple and easy to do. If you are known to everyone as Jo or Joe, perhaps you want to go more formal, and now become Joann or Joseph. Your brother and your great-aunt will always know you as Jo, or perhaps Jo Jo, or Joey, but in a business world, perhaps a more formal name will suit you better in your next role. Introduce yourself as Joseph or Joann, and people will quickly change to that.

Perhaps you were always eager to speak up and be the first to offer an opinion. In a planning meeting, the first person to venture an opinion is setting himself or herself up to be shot down or shot up, depending on the character of the meeting. Perhaps it is time to change that habit. Do not be the first to offer an opinion. Always listen to one or two other opinions and consider them well before speaking your mind. People who know you and work with you every day will notice the difference almost immediately. There is a downside. Someone else may get credit for an opinion that you share, and nobody will know you deserve the credit. More likely, you will become known as a person who considers a problem carefully from all sides before commenting. A simple change can produce big results.

How do you respond to bad news? Are you stoic and strong, or do you fall apart? Regardless of your answer, is it working well for you? If not, change it. Be aware of who you are and how you are perceived.

When you were growing up, you made several big

life changes, going from elementary school to junior high to high school. The people who were important and looked up to in each school setting changed over time. You may have known many of these people for the twelve years from first grade through senior year of high school, and yet they never made an impression on you until the last two years of high school.

What worked well for you in elementary school did not work in high school. We all make changes over time, and we all reinvent ourselves and adapt to new environments. Instead of just responding to the new environment, this time you can plan how you want to be perceived, and you can reinvent yourself. Keep at it, and you will be amazed at how quickly the new you will emerge. Remember that life philosophy? As you reinvent yourself, you will adjust and grow. And your life philosophy will expand in the process.

I had the good fortune to work with several really great people at different times in my career. Either I would move to another company, or they would. We would both end up at a third company and start working together again. In one case, it was a very big company, and both of us had left the original company and moved hundreds of miles. We had both started working for the new company at about the same time but in different cities and different product lines. We met one day at a meeting and got together after the meeting to compare notes.

We reminisced about certain characters we had worked with originally. It is a really small world in business. The same people keep coming back into our business spheres, either with our company or maybe with a competitor. Several of the people we talked about had been through very dramatic and even traumatic life circumstances. We talked about mutual acquaintances that we worked with at different times, and I was impressed that her impression of a person sometimes was exactly the same as mine but occasionally much different. In one case, she had known this person before he reinvented himself, and I met him after the new person emerged. She thought he was a perfect fool, and I thought he was a really powerful leader and a person of great integrity. It was hard to believe that we were talking about the same person. Reinvention is possible, and it can be powerful.

Most people do not need to reinvent themselves so dramatically. But a little fine-tuning never hurts. While you are developing your plan, take time to think about how you would like to be perceived by your colleagues and friends. What can you do to improve on your basic qualities and traits?

14

Ups and Downs

Most people have ups and downs in their daily lives. At times of stress, the ups still occur, but they do not seem to produce the same happiness and joy, and the downs seem to be magnified. Despite your best efforts, there will be some periods of anxiety and emotional fatigue. When that emotional fatigue increases, elements of depression can set in. This is life.

We talked about ways to conserve your emotional energy and about when to seek help for signs of depression. But on a day-to-day basis, you should try to restore congruence to your life and your daily routine. It helps you to keep focused.

You have a lot to do just to develop your plan and execute it. You need to reach out to possible contacts and check the job boards. This daily work process becomes your occupation for the moment.

Ask yourself what you are doing, and how you will measure your success. Refer to your plan, which by now should be well defined.

My job is to find a good position, one where I can feel fulfilled and comfortable. My goal is to find a place to use my considerable talent, to be successful, and to keep moving on my career path. This is your short-term goal and your daily focus.

Against this laudable process, there are negative forces pushing from time to time, and sometimes every day. If you are out of work, how are the bills getting paid? The longer you are out of work, the more financial pressure you will have. The longer you do not have that next position, the more your feelings of self-worth and self-esteem are subject to attack by doubt and fear.

Remember those issues from Chapter 6. Events will happen in the course of a day that may trigger some of those issues and cause you to dwell on them. Even though you have had initial success dealing with them, they will come back, like a swarm of hungry mosquitoes, sucking your emotional energy. Why did this happen? It is not fair.

While you need to critically assess and reassess your situation, and measure the success of your plan over time, the longer it takes to find that new position, the more often you will have pangs of doubt and anxiety.

The congruence that develops when you have a good position with a solid company is a silent strength. When it is not there, you will be vulnerable to a variety of conflicts and dissonance that you did not notice before.

That is what I mean by ups and downs. They are times of happiness, joy, and peace interspersed between times of stress and anxiety. Talking with a favorite neighbor across the backyard fence on a warm spring day is a joy—a happy time. Then a friend calls and tells you that they are getting a divorce, or maybe your spouse calls and tells you that the car will not start. These are not overwhelming things, but when you have multiple events occurring in the same day, it can feel like a roller-coaster ride. Realize that this is no different than it was when you were employed. It is your reaction to the event that is different. If you have too many negative events in a day, you need some positive events to balance the day.

You can create a positive event anytime you wish. Give someone a smile. Do something good for someone who does not expect it. Call your mom, or your brother or sister, and see how he or she is doing, especially if you have not seen that person in a while.

If you call a relative or friend, he or she will undoubtedly ask you how you are doing. Be ready for this. Remember to tell your loved one that you are really doing fine. You have time to relax and reflect. Most times that will be the truth. Yes, you are calling that person because today has been a little tough, but overall, you really are doing well. Again, don't give the friend or relative a blow-by-blow description of everything that has happened in the last forty-eight hours. That will just exhaust you and drain him or her. You are calling to replenish your emotional energy, not drain it.

Read a book, or research something online that interests you. Go for a walk. See a movie, but select a lighthearted one rather than a suspense thriller.

Movies can affect you, and a suspense thriller may actually drain your emotional energy. Build or create something. Complete a chore that you have been putting off for the right time. Get into the project, and feel the positive feelings of accomplishment. Spend time with family or friends. Recharge your emotional energy batteries. Figure out what has been draining your energy, and determine what you can do about it.

Circumstances like this show what you are made of. And you are made of strong stuff. Say it again and again until you really believe it. You are made of strong stuff. Yes, that is self-talk, and it works.

Many people in this world would trade places with you. There are people who suffer with physical and mental issues, and people who ache from the strain of taking care of an invalid relative. They might think you have it pretty easy. Perhaps you could even help them in some way. If you lose yourself in someone else's struggles, your pain does not seem as awful.

Or just be nice to people that you meet. Have a kind word for everyone. Smiles will come back to you and make you feel better. You have to start it. Give one, and get one or two back.

When you feel good, you are less prone to colds and flu. When you exercise regularly and eat right, you feel better. This is simple stuff and very powerful. Put in the time every day doing what you need to do to promote your job search. Then spend part of the day getting away from that and helping others less fortunate. If we all did that, we might attain world peace. We would definitely make the world a better place.

15

What Does It All Mean?

We have covered a lot of ground, and not in great detail. This book covers the highlights and depends on your natural skills and abilities and life experiences to help you to understand. These are simple concepts. Some of them will come very naturally, and others will not. If any of these ideas seem foreign, do some research to learn more.

Many years ago, I used a personal organization system called Daytimers. There was a process described in the program that showed you how to organize your time and your life. I carried a little book in the inside pocket of my suit coat that had separate pages for each day of the month. I kept the books for past months in a plastic storage box, so I could refer to previous notes whenever needed.

There was a book for each month, and you bought a new set of books each year. Every day, you tore off the perforated top corner of the page, so you could easily turn to the page for the current day to make your notes. There were several organizational systems out there, and they were all very similar. Each night, you reviewed the day and made plans for the next day. The system also included a contact list, with names and addresses and phone numbers.

This system worked quite well, allowing me to handle multiple issues each day and keep multiple projects moving. Today, we have MS Outlook and similar programs to help us to organize our time. It coordinates our work on the computer, tablet, and smartphone, and carries tasks forward to the next day, and our Outlook can interact with others directly to set up meetings or share information. We have external support devices that allow us to record ideas, facts, schedules, and experiences. And we have our smartphone cameras. A picture is worth a thousand words sometimes. If you are not working, maybe you no longer have this level of organization. A simple daily calendar or planner can really help. Most people have cell phones that can handle a calendar program and task list. Although it seems old-fashioned, a paper process works very well if you do not want to invest in the computer program. However you choose to do it, you need to be organized. You have a lot of things to do.

If you take time to commit your ideas and plans to some type of permanent record, and if you take time to update those records and plans, you will learn a lot about how your mind works and about how you process information and ideas. While you have the time, you can learn interesting things about yourself.

For years, people have assumed that a person had to multitask every day and be able to move from one issue or idea to another rapidly and then go back to that issue later. A common comment heard every day was that a person was doing ten things at once. I wondered about that observation. We were all proud of our ability to multitask. Looking back, I believe we were fooling ourselves and often spinning our wheels.

Many people believe that a person can work on only one thing at a time and that we lose time and expend extra energy when we have to switch gears to move from one task to another multiple times in a workday. Gary Keller and Jay Papasan wrote a *New York Times* bestseller book, *The One Thing*, about this. (See "Resources" section.) It is difficult to keep focused when we are distracted by multiple tasks. Interruptions occur in every workday that require us to drop what we are doing and get back to it later. You lose time when you have to drop what you are doing and look at something else. Very often, another person's poor planning becomes your emergency and takes your precious time and energy. The ability to remain flexible becomes a virtue in the business world. You have to handle issues and problems in multiple areas. But you cannot multitask really big issues. You may get through the fire drill, but it will not be your best work. Really big issues require your complete attention and focus. Otherwise, you may lose track of details and feel scattered and frazzled.

When you have a huge project, you have to break it down into smaller units, and eventually into individual tasks that must often be performed in a specific order to keep a project moving. Your present opportunity is like that. And you can focus better and plan better when you are not multitasking with ten projects at a time. Decide on your priorities. Limit your focus to the important stuff. Organize your work and your workday to accomplish your goals.

We have discussed a process that starts with self-inventory, self-awareness, and self-discovery. Look at all the parts of your life and understand the interactions between internal and external factors, competing priorities, and unexpected delays and unforeseen circumstances. All of these things put together produce a complex daily schedule of planning, execution, assessment, and revised planning, new execution, and reassessment. The fact that you are not working may change your priorities a little, but life goes on, and you have a lot to do to just keep up.

This is hard and sometimes perplexing work. It is difficult to do it effectively when you are disorganized and tired. Keep it as simple and regular as you can, and you will get a lot more accomplished.

Stay organized and stay focused. Be sensitive to external and internal changes that may affect your plans. You may be able to accomplish more than one goal in a day, but be wary of overextending when you are multitasking. Look for opportunities to help others along the way, and still stay focused on your important goals. Helping others helps to recharge the emotional energy in your soul.

Doing ten things poorly is rarely as good as doing two things well and putting the other eight off for another day. Getting every project done "just in time" rarely shows your true ability. Good organization and planning your day allow you to accomplish so much more, usually with higher-quality work output overall.

Remember that this is truly an opportunity to take stock of your life situation and improve it. When life gives you lemons, make lemonade. Even in stressful times, there are opportunities. In fact, stressful times probably have more opportunities hidden within the multiple interactions that will occur in your day than nonstressful days. *But nonstressful days give you the opportunity to relax and reflect.*

You are not alone, and you are not the first person to walk this path. Many resources are available to you. In fact, there are so many resources and opportunities that you need to be very picky, using your goals to decide which will be most helpful to you.

Believe in yourself, and others will believe in you. A good idea at a bad time is really a bad idea (at that time). If the time is not right, you will not be successful. But there may be a better time coming, so don't throw the idea away. We live in a country with more personal freedom than any other country in the world or any other time in history. Enjoy it. A lot of things are possible.

My father used to say that every five-year life segment produces significant changes in a person's life and in a person's outlook on life. It was an observation from his life and his experience and observations of others. Where were you five years ago? What has changed? Where will you be in the next five years?

Keep your life as simple and uncomplicated as you can, especially in this time of stress. A simple plan is easier to change as external circumstances or internal ideas evolve. You need to include enough detail (and complexity) to make it comprehensive. Many factors compete or complicate the two or three main factors that you are focused on. You may need to add some extra considerations to make the plan more realistic. But nobody can handle twenty subplots to the main plot. Keeping it simple decreases your overall stress levels.

When you finally land, and you get that next dream job or find a good replacement for the job you no longer have, use the experience you obtained and the lessons you learned to be a better person, a better parent, or a better child or sibling. Remember those who helped you, and look for opportunities to pay it forward.

I hope my little book has given you some assistance in navigating through these difficult times. Now get out there and live life to the fullest, and if you have a bad day, pick yourself up, figure out how to get back on track, and keep moving forward. Read or review any or all of the chapters of this book. Although the book is short and easy to read, *you may find new ideas the second time through.*

Try to learn something new every day, and try to do something positive for yourself and for at least one other person every day, even if it is only to give them a smile or a pat on the back or a helping hand.

16

Being the Best You Can Be—Self-Actualization

While we are discussing self-talk, self-esteem, and related subjects, I would like to introduce a discussion of self-actualization. If you Google the word, there is a definition that comes up first that states:

> Self-actualization is the realization or fulfillment of one's talents and potentialities, especially considered as a drive or need present in everyone.

The term was first introduced by Kurt Goldstein, who described it as the motive that propelled a person to realize his or her full potential. Abraham Maslow used the term in a paper in 1943, "A Theory of Human Motivation," to describe the top level of his Human Needs Pyramid. The first four levels of the Hierarchy of Needs Pyramid went from physiological needs, to safety needs, to love/belonging needs, to esteem, and the top level was self-actualization, which was described as a drive present in everyone to realize their top talents and potentialities. The first four levels were called deficiency needs, and if these were not met, the person would feel anxiety and tension. Only if the lower needs were met could a person focus on the higher levels and achieve self-actualization and find fulfillment. Maslow published his book, *Motivation and Personality*, in 1954, and introduced the term metamotivation to describe people who go beyond the basic needs and strive for constant betterment.

Business management theorists quote Maslow's "Hierarchy of Needs" frequently. This is certainly a description of intense self-motivation. It has been said that all motivation is self-motivation. Self-motivation is very important, and it certainly describes internal motivation. But there is also external motivation, like monthly bills piling up and loved ones expressing their dependency on you and expectations of others in general.

As Maslow described, basic needs must be met before an individual can focus on the higher needs. But when those lower needs are met, self-actualization or self-motivation to attain one's highest potential can be a powerful force. Maslow's theory focused on "intensity at a task." The greater the motivation, the more intensely one will perform a specific task.

What are your "potentialities"? What are you capable of accomplishing? What do you want to accomplish? Why do you want to accomplish these things? And is it worth the time and effort it will take?

You have to be practical, but you have to dream a little here and stretch a little too. If you do not set stretch goals, you will not accomplish nearly as much. Maybe you are in a middle management position, but you want to be the CEO someday. Is this realistic? If so, what do you need to do to get there? Do you have the desire to do this? It will not be easy. But it could be very worthwhile. What will it take? Will it conflict with other dreams, desires, or important goals to which you are already committed? If you are devoted to your family, is it realistic to think that you can become the CEO and still have time for your family? If the CEO role seems too all-consuming, perhaps there is another senior role that would fit your overall life goals better.

What is most important to you? How can you incorporate new goals and desires into your current life equation? What will you have to give up?

What about competing priorities? It would be nice to be able to focus on the job at hand and not worry about other things. But we all have competing priorities. When you are at work, you want to focus all your attentions on your job. But if you have other stresses, and if those stresses are causing acute strife, you undoubtedly will find yourself thinking about those other stresses and not putting 100 percent into the job. Likewise after work, when you should be able to focus on the family, or the project at hand, work issues may push into your subconscious and even your conscious thoughts.

Since you are not working presently, how will you use your time wisely? You certainly have competing priorities, including food, clothing, shelter, and expectations of others. Finding the right position becomes urgent. It is also important, but it may stack up differently against other priorities in the urgent list vs. the important list. It might be the most important priority you have, but not the most urgent. At times, you might feel it is the most urgent, but not the most important.

There is a real difference between urgent issues and important issues. And there are times when you will decide that one is more pressing than the other. If it is urgent and important, you will probably do that first. But what if something is urgent, like a phone ringing, and you will not know if it is important until you answer it? Is it important to stop what you are doing and answer that phone? What if it is the boss, with more information about the question you are researching? What if it is a salesman who wants to sell you timeshares in the islands? You make decisions on urgent and important every day, and you make them automatically for the most part. Many people answer the ringing phone, and they lose time if it is not important. There is no right or wrong here. You can focus only on the important and ignore the urgent. Or you can focus less on the urgent and more on the important. The balance point is yours to establish and maintain. And you do it every day.

129

Back to self-actualization. Do you know yourself? Do you have a realistic view of your abilities and capabilities? Is there congruency between your picture of yourself and the way others see you? Are you capable of working at a higher level of efficiency and effectiveness?

If you have been writing down your original ideas, the first plan, and subsequent changes and additions, you may want to read over this material. Do you see anything worth going back for a second look? Are you pleased with your current plan? Is it working for you? How do you know?

When you find the next position, put all of the materials into a folder and label it "My Goals and Ideas," or "The Plan." Put it away for a while. You will have enough to do with the new position. You want to learn as much as you can in a short period of time and get back on top of your game. But all of the thinking, planning, and decision-making that you have done is worth keeping and returning to from time to time. And all the good habits you cultivated in this important growth period should be valued and continued if possible. This was hard work. This was worthwhile work.

Keep your tools in good working order. Your most powerful tool is your active mind. Your active mind is like a saw. If you keep it sharp, it will do a better job, and you will get more done with less time and effort. How do you keep your mind sharp?

Your mind is linked to your body intimately. If you are exercising, getting enough sleep, relaxing, taking in new information to expand your horizons, and challenging yourself to use and develop your talents and abilities, your intellectual capacity will increase. Multiple body systems will be in balance, and your hormones will give you a sense of well-being. This is part of self-actualization also.

When you are not working, the television can become an inviting time-filler. Actually, it is probably a time-waster. Reruns of old sitcoms do not contribute much to increasing your intellectual capacity. If there is a movie that you always wanted to see, that is a different story. You might want to save it on the DVR if you have that capacity, so you can see it on your schedule, and fast-forward through the commercials.

You may want to watch the news, or you may want to just relax a little after spending all day researching job leads. But be wary of long periods in front of the TV. Your brain and your bottom will both become numb.

Hobbies and exercise activities are great to sharpen the mind and reduce stress. But your major focus right now is finding that next position or starting your new company or whatever your plan says. And *that has to be your primary priority each day.*

The internet is a great source of information. It also can be a big time-waster. When you find something that catches your attention, you click on it, and read the article, or start the video or the slideshow. An hour later, you have surfed through sixteen different sites, and you still have not started the important research that you wanted to accomplish today.

Learn to control the mouse clicks. Be more time-conscious. Spend five minutes, not one hour, on something that catches your eye. And do not move from that first item to two or three more.

There are multiple questions in this chapter—more

than in the rest of the entire book. They are questions that can empower you to move forward. There are no right or wrong answers, only answers that will allow you to reach your potentialities. I would encourage you to read this chapter again after you have completed the book. The opportunity that you now have is not only to find a job to replace the one you had. The opportunity here is to identify the path that will take you to another higher level of success and fulfillment.

You have undoubtedly learned something about yourself in this process. And you probably have changed a little. If you reach the level of self-actualization, you will see things differently. You will evaluate new ideas and situations differently. You will work more efficiently and effectively. Keep on track, and follow your plan.

17

As Your Energy Returns

Stressful times will cause you to become very tired—emotionally and often physically. Perhaps you are not sleeping well at night. Your established routine has been severely disrupted. Worry and doubt can sneak up on even the strongest person and drain your batteries.

Your "emotional batteries" are constantly recharging in a healthy, positive life. You normally do not have to be concerned with your energy levels. You wake up refreshed in the morning, ready to go to work, have a productive day at work, come home after work, enjoy some activities for your personal and family life in the evening, and go to bed comfortably tired and fall asleep easily. This is the ideal pattern that we may actually have at times. But you are not in normal times now. Your job is gone, you have multiple stresses pulling at you, and the daily patterns are gone.

The stressful time you are now in is very similar to running a marathon. Just as you tire initially in a long race, you have to learn to conserve energy, adjust your stride, and settle in for the long haul. The difference is that you train for a marathon and get conditioned over time. You did not have that time to prepare for the current race you are in. So what can you do?

First and foremost, keep track of your emotional energy. Do things that recharge your batteries. Avoid things that unnecessarily drain your emotional reserves. It sounds easy, and it is, but you can easily drain your emotional energy to a critical point and not realize it until you start feeling bad.

Stop dwelling on what happened. Yes, we know it was not fair. We already settled that in the first part of the book. Most people are able to turn off the video in their minds, but there are triggers that will restart it, and you may not be aware until you see that video playing over and over several times in your mind, and then you realize that you have been draining your battery unnecessarily. This is just not productive. If it helped, I would suggest doing it every day. If it does not help at all, and it rarely does, then stop doing it. Learn to turn it off, and figure out ways to change your environment, change your daily schedule, and change your thought patterns. Do something different. Do whatever it takes to stop draining your batteries.

We talked about self-talk. Positive self-talk will actually help you to remain positive and avoid the negative doldrums that rob you of energy. Make an effort to be nice to someone every day, whether it is just a smile or a kind word, or perform random acts of kindness to friends and strangers. You feel good about yourself when you see that you have made a positive difference in someone's day.

This book has recommended several times that you take stock of your current situation and plan your next steps. Normally, that is a good thing. But if you have not found a new position after several months and your money is running out, you may find yourself thinking about this repeatedly throughout the day and becoming anxious each time.

Anxiety can motivate people to make changes. If someone is coming after you with a club, anxiety can make your feet run faster and allow you to run farther. Adrenalin can be a wonderful thing. But if anxiety about finding a job makes you release adrenalin, and there is no crisis to run from or fight to be had, the anxiety disturbs your sleep and invades your productive day. The adrenalin release causes you to feel more anxious. It is a vicious escalating cycle.

Discounting is a related issue of which you should be aware. Discounting occurs when you evaluate a really positive event as not relevant or not as important as a negative event that occurred the same day. If you discount the good and positive events, and you dwell on the negative events, you will drain your batteries dry, and you will become emotionally tired, and perhaps depressed.

Depression can be insidious, or it can be overwhelming and sudden. Many people carry some depression with them for years, or even a lifetime. They learn to cope with it. There are many ways to help yourself out of depression, but stress, illness, disturbed sleep, and negative events can adversely affect even the strongest person and bring anyone back down.

If you are physically very tired, you may feel depressed because of it. Physical fatigue can be treated with a few good nights of sleep, or even some naps in the afternoon, if you have time. During stressful times, I advised my patients struggling with ongoing depression to not do so much physically that they become overtired. Fatigue is fatigue, and physical fatigue and emotional fatigue feel very similar to many people. If you cannot sleep, or the fatigue persists, see your doctor.

Fatigue can be a symptom of a serious disease process. Depending on your symptoms, the doctor may want to check your blood sugar, your cholesterol, your kidney function, your heart, your digestive system, your thyroid, your adrenal function, etc. A checkup is the place to start. If all of that is normal, could it just be stress? If you know it is stress, or highly suspect it, what do you do about it?

Plan your day so that you are comfortably tired at bedtime, and try to have a regular bedtime. If you take a four-hour nap in the afternoon because you are bored, you probably will not sleep well that night. There is nothing wrong with a nap. Make it a shorter one, so you sleep at night.

If you do all of this successfully, and you feel your emotional energy returning, your positive attitude will be evident to you and others. Bolster this change with an increase in your regular physical exercise. Don't overdo it. Just increase your activity a little each day. Exercise releases endorphins, those wonderful natural substances that give you a sense of well-being. As your energy improves, your attitude will become more positive. The old you that everyone knows and loves will become the predominant you each day.

Use this positive attitude, this renewed energy. Do whatever you can to keep it going. Guard it from forces that can take you backward. Watch out especially for negative people and unnecessary drama.

When I was in practice, a few patients in my practice were continually and abysmally negative. They were such downers that the staff complained every time they saw certain names on the schedule. We actually tried to not schedule these people on the same day, because two of them in a row could ruin the day for everyone.

I questioned one of these people about their attitude one day, and I will never forget the response. This patient had complained about my receptionist, the color of my tie, an original watercolor painting in the reception area that a patient had done for our office, and the temperature of the waiting room. And that was all done in two sentences, without taking a breath. I asked her why she came back to our office if she was so dissatisfied with just about everything about our office. She looked at me in surprise and then became alarmed.

Her answer really surprised me. I may be paraphrasing a little, but it went something like this. "Oh, Doctor, don't get upset with me, and please don't take me too seriously. I am sorry if I offended you. You and your staff treat me really well, and you are so courteous and friendly. I feel better than I have in years since I started coming here. I like you as my doctor, because you listen to your patients. I tell all my friends that." I smiled, and she seemed relieved.

141

The next thing she said made all of us speechless. "I hope you will not throw me out of the practice. My last doctor did that. When you tell me to come back in a month, I try to figure out a way to come in at least once between visits. I feel good when I am here. I don't mean anything by my comments. I just talk a lot, and I complain a lot when I am nervous. I get lonely, and your people are so nice."

She mentioned my receptionist by name, as someone she felt especially close to. This was the receptionist that she complained about several minutes before. She did not remember complaining about her.

Then she added, "You should see how my dentist treats me. He is so mean. Sometimes I think he wants me to leave the practice. Sometimes he tells me to get out and not come back. But I do come back, and I watch what I say, and it gets better."

I wanted to inquire why she was so negative all the time, but I thought it might be wise to not open that door right then, in case I could not close it. Things improved immediately after that. The staff did not complain so much about her after that. Her negativity was just learned behavior. We learned to adapt, and she improved over time, at least in her visits to my office. You could call it cognitive therapy, but I think it was just better understanding of this person and realizing she was doing the best she could.

The point of this story is that this patient was a person that would drain your emotional energy to nothing if you were under stress and were around her every day. We had to be aware at all times that she could be exasperating. We learned to not respond to her comments, and she learned to stop making so many negative comments. I think we changed as much as she did.

If you have someone like that in your life, be aware. Try not to respond to the negativity. And I would suggest that you not argue with such a person on any point that carries a lot of emotional energy for either of you. The best of days can be ruined by such an encounter. If this is a loved one in your immediate family, you may have to be involved more frequently. But pick your battles. Keep your energy reserves up to optimal levels as much as you can. It makes a difference.

18

Putting It All Together

So now you have had the quick tour. You are over the shock, and you no longer feel sorry for yourself. You have perspective. If you do slip back, you know how to identify it and how to get yourself back on track. You have or will soon have a working plan, and you are working it. You have marshaled your support and incorporated your family and friends into your plan. You have your faith and good self-esteem, and you have made important decisions to guide your efforts. In short, you have a comprehensive plan. You may not have all of this, but you have most of it, and enough of it to get moving.

Now is the time for action. This is hard work. Hard work is good for you. You will discover along the way some wonderful things that you overlooked before.

You will see changes in your life that will amaze you. Almost all of those changes will be for the good. If they are not, stop and take another look at the plan. Look for the good in every day.

For those people who are interested, the next chapter talks about life coaching. In a previous position with a very excellent company, I was afforded a business coach. I was relatively new in the role of chief medical officer of a large health plan, and my boss wanted me to succeed. He convinced the board of directors to pay for a business coach, and I am forever grateful. My business coach was as much a life coach as a business coach, and she helped me to become a much better leader.

She told me that she only asked the questions. I had to come up with the answers, and my answers then had to be put into actions, and changes had to be made that would help me obtain better results. We talked twice per month in the beginning and then once a month for another year. Over time, I began to look forward to our discussions. I chose the topic each time. She asked questions to clarify the issues, or to understand why I wanted her help on an issue. Our discussions were very focused. We did not discuss the weather or current events the way two friends might interact. She questioned even the most simple comment or decision sometimes. She was not critical of the decision. She wanted me to understand why I made the decision that I did, and what effect that one decision would have on other parts of the business. In the same way, a life coach can help you to better understand where you are, how you got there, and in some cases, what you need to do to change the paradigm. But you answer the questions, and you decide the best answer. After all, it is your life.

I asked one of my favorite life coaches for comments about coaching. She helped me to describe life coaching in the next chapter and how it can help you to be a better person and to focus on finding the new position you are looking for. In other words, how can you take advantage of this opportunity that you have been given?

There are some other life coaching resources listed at the end of this book. I hope you will find them interesting and worthwhile.

Remember that your present circumstance was not caused by you. You did not do anything wrong, and even if you have identified things that you want to change for the future, those things did not make your job situation happen. This is your opportunity to change your life and change your future.

I encourage you to make the world a better place along the way. Find resources that will help you to get to your next position in life. Help others to see how they can be successful in their lives. Success is not necessarily power, prestige, or money. Success is finding happiness, contentment, peace, and joy, and doing it with integrity and purpose. Remember that life is a journey and not a destination.

What an opportunity you have been given.

19

Life Coaching, Counseling, and Resources

Don't be afraid to ask for help when you need it. These are stressful times. There are so many re-sources available to you, and some work better than others. But they are not one size fits all. And it can be difficult sometimes to tell what you need.

Many people underestimate the severity of their dys-function. Dysfunction is a terrible-sounding word, but it simply means your source of pain.

Is something bothering you other than the job loss? Are you depressed? Are you anxious? Are you still hurting from some other life situation, or do you have health issues? If so, see your doctor. Based on your doctor's exam, you may benefit from seeing a counselor. Unload the burdens that you can unload. *The future belongs to you. Prepare for it.*

If you are overtly depressed, not sleeping, not feeling happy even when something really positive happens (a process known as anhedonia), you should definitely see a doctor or counselor. If you have any suicidal thoughts or ideation, get help immediately.

What if you are not having these kinds of symptoms, but you are just contemplating the future, and you want to delve more deeply into some aspects of your life and your current situation. Consider life coaching. You do not have to be hurting to see a life coach. You just have to be interested in assessing and perhaps changing your direction.

There are resources on life coaching listed in the "References" section at the end of the book. I have a very good friend who is a certified life coach. Let me share what she told me. She has a good perspective on this.

Life coaching is not therapy, and it is not consultation. There are professionals who do both therapy and life coaching, but they are different disciplines, with different outcomes. If you need therapy, you must do that first. Therapy takes a person from a place of brokenness to a place of wholeness. Life coaching takes a person from a place of wholeness to a place of excellence. A life coach does not give you "expert" advice like a consultant might do. A life coach asks empowering questions. You answer those questions in a confidential, comfortable environment, and work on ways to sharpen your abilities and achieve the desired outcomes.

A life coach will hold you accountable for deciding what you want to do, where you want to go, and how to get there. Once you decide, the life coach helps you set up boundaries, reframe processes, and explore your options. *Life coaching is based on your ideas, your decisions, and your vision for success.*

There is a phrase that sums this up, and I could not find the person who first said this to give proper attribution. It goes like this:

It is not about the thing. What is the thing behind the thing?

Some of you may be familiar with executive coaching and may have worked with an executive coach somewhere along the way. An executive coach works in a very similar manner to a life coach but focusing on the business environment.

You may be the last person in the room to realize that you need help. Your family and friends may be reluctant to tell you. But if there seems to be an elephant in the room, and nobody wants to talk about it, it might be you. Take note, and find time to ask about it when you are in a comfortable, confidential surrounding with someone you know and respect, who will tell you what others may be afraid to say. Please try not to kill the messenger, or even argue with this individual. Critical comment from someone who cares about you is the greatest gift you can receive. It is hard to receive without responding, but much harder to give. If you respond in a hostile manner, you will never receive that gift again.

Remember that you learn most from someone who sees things differently than you do. If ten people in a room all have exactly the same idea and see things the same, there is no learning that can take place with discussion. But if one person has a very different take, it may be wise to listen, because you may learn so much more and be able to see things from a different perspective.

Life is a continual journey of discovery.

So,

You have this opportunity.

What will you do about it?

To My Readers

I hope you found some benefit in reading my book. I am interested in your comments. Did the book help you to find a new and better position? Did you find practical information that helped you get going again? Do you have suggestions to make it better?

Please visit my website, http://DrBobRobison.com. My website was set up to give us a forum to discuss how to make the most of the opportunity you have when you are terminated for whatever reason. I will try to address all reasonable concerns or questions, either individually, or on the website forum. Use the contact form to send me ideas, comments, and suggestions.

Have a great day and a wonderful rest of your life. And make the most of this opportunity.

—Bob

Resources

- International Coach Federation, headquartered in Lexington, KY. Check their website: https://coachfederation.org/. At this site, you can learn more about life coaching and the standards that life coaches work under, and you can also find certified life coaches in your area.

- Drucker, Peter F. *The Practice of Management.* Harper Collins, 1954.

- Burns, David D. *Feeling Good: the New Mood Therapy.* This book has helped many people understand depression and has shown how to improve your perspective on life. It explains cognitive behavioral therapy and teaches you how to dig out of the hole that we call depression.

- Google. <u>www.google.com.</u> There are so many resources available online that will help you write a better resume, prepare for an interview, and find a new position. Once you are ready, spend some time each day working your plan and deciding how best to find your next opportunity. Don't let anything or anyone stop you. You are on your way.

- Keller, Gary, and Jay Papasan. *The One Thing*. Rellek Publishing Partners, 2002.

- <u>http://DrBobRobison.com</u>, my website, set up to interact with you and take your suggestions and ideas.

- Look in a good mirror and smile at the person you see. You are your best resource, and you will get it done.

Illustration—Start to Plan

Taking notes, from Chapter 5, "The Difference between Static and Disaster."

Write down your thoughts, organize them, and discuss them with significant people in your life who will be affected by the decisions you make. Write down enough comments that the plan begins to have a clear form. A plan starts to take shape quickly, and each day brings new questions or new decisions. This is your part of the equation—the factors you can anticipate and control. Multiple options may require a Plan B or Plan C.

Day 1 observations

I am well known in my industry. I should look at associated industries, perhaps.

I have always respected the people from XYZ

Corporation. They are knowledgeable, and they seem satisfied to be working for this company. Maybe I should check out possible opportunities, even if I have to start at a lower level. Who do I know that works there? Maybe John Smith would have a contact there. I think he worked for them in the past.

I am angry. How could they do this to me, after all I did for that company?

If I have to move, what effect will that have for my family? Will my kids want to move to a new city? My father-in-law is not in good health. What if something happens to him? We might have a long trip home. Maybe I should look for something within one hundred miles of my present location.

How did this happen? I had no idea they would eliminate my job. This makes no sense. I wonder if one of my colleagues stabbed me in the back to protect his position. Even if he did, it is over now. Move on.

I had a great team. I wonder how they are doing. I wonder if they will reach out. Should I reach out to them?

I am so exhausted. I will try to get to bed at a decent hour tonight.

What resources are out there? What should I do first? Why did this happen to me, and why now? Things were going so well.

I bet it was Francis. He never did like me. I don't like him much either. I don't think he knows what he is doing. Ah, well, not my problem now.

I need a break. I am going to go to the movies and buy a big bucket of popcorn and see a movie. I will not go to the Alfred Hitchcock movie marathon. Maybe a lighthearted comedy.

It is a nice day. I think I will go for a walk in the park nearby.

Day 3

I slept better last night. I needed that.

Wow, so many of my team members and colleagues called, including two who were laid off with me. What a day that was. My boss was a real jerk. He knew this was happening but gave me no time to get used to the idea. And I did so much for him.

I don't feel like starting my job search today. And I surely do not want to look at my finances today. I may spend the day in bed. No, my back hurts. I need to get up and do something.

Why did this happen? My kids are upset, but they said they understand we may have to move.

I think I want to talk with Pastor Tom. He always seems to have such a positive outlook.

I think I am gaining weight. I need to watch that.

Next Monday, I will start my job search. I will make a list of possible companies to look at, and see who I might know. I have not looked at LinkedIn for a long time. I need to see what others see when they look me up.

Where do I go from here?

Day 7

I seem to be okay. I have read twelve chapters of Dr.

Bob's book in the last week. Maybe I should finish that today.

I have a list of possible companies that are in this area. I contacted several recruiters that I know.

Today, I made a list of the companies across the country that I know something about that I would like to work for. Tomorrow, I will add bookmarks for all of them and start reviewing the websites. I will select the top ten and make it a point to check each of them twice weekly. I will check the next twenty once weekly. My wife and I decided that we will stay on this side of the Mississippi River for right now.

I really enjoyed working out in the yard. I have not had the time to do that for several years. That old job was a real killer. I am not sorry to see that stress go away. Maybe this was not such a bad thing.

I have the start of my plan. My father-in-law says that he is doing well and not to worry about him. I knew he would say that, and it is reasonable. But I will still try to stay close to here. I have a meeting set up with Claire. She works for ABC Corporation, and they have a big office here in town. I checked out their website.

There are several jobs listed there. Maybe she knows someone.

Pastor Tom was a big help. I knew he would be.

I need to talk to our financial planner. We should be okay. I want to be sure. I want to prepare for the next six months. It will take that long to find a good position.

Note

At this point, it is time to start formalizing a plan. You have good ideas and a place to start. Write it down (or do it on the computer, so you can edit it easily) and review it. The shock is over, and the bills are going to start coming in. There is a balance between simple and complete. Simple is good, but complexities at least need to be outlined, so you do not lose track of them.

Get the resume out, and go over it. You will need to send off resumes very soon. Get that resume up to date, and decide how to describe your recent termination. That will be the first thing they see in your job history.

Develop your story. Adjust or reinvent yourself as you see fit. Be in touch with your emotional energy, and keep your batteries charged. Smile at others to receive a smile back. When someone asks how you are, tell them you are fine and working hard to find a new position. And be fine. You will get through this the same way that hundreds of other people get through it every day. Planning and putting some time in now will pay off big for you in the future.

About the Plan

There is no sample plan in this resource area. That is by design. Your plan is as unique as your planning process. Your plan could be something as simple as:

- Limit the target area to within fifty miles of present location. Family responsibilities require that.

- Will work in banking, financial services, or similar businesses.

- Make a list of all businesses that meet this description, and check their websites or job lists twice weekly. Call five recruiters that I know, and send them my resume, after it has been redone.

Consider management positions at midlevel or senior level.

- Complexities would be added when there are responsibilities with aging parents, children with special needs, spouse has good position, social or civic responsibilities ongoing, etc.

- Review plan in a month, if nothing definite has come through.

So you have this opportunity. What now?

Take care. Thank you for listening and learning.

Bob